Politicking

Politicking

How to Get Elected,
Take Action, and Make an
Impact in Your Community

BILL RAUCH

Farrar, Straus and Giroux / NEW YORK

FARRAR, STRAUS AND GIROUX
19 Union Square West, New York 10003

Distributed in Canada by Douglas & McIntyre Ltd.
Printed in the United States of America
FIRST EDITION, 2004

Library of Congress Cataloging-in-Publication Data
Rauch, William.
    Politicking : how to get elected, take action, and make an impact in
your community / Bill Rauch.— 1st ed.
        p.   cm.
    ISBN 0-374-27855-5 (hardcover : alk. paper)
1. Rauch, William.   2. Mayors—South Carolina—Beaufort—Biography.
3. Political culture—South Carolina—Beaufort.   4. Beaufort (S.C.)—
Politics and government.   5. Press secretaries—New York (State)—
New York—Biography.   6. Koch, Ed, 1924–   —Friends and associates.
7. Political culture—New York (State)—New York.   8. New York
(N.Y.)—Politics and government—1951–   9. Politics, Practical—
United States—Case studies.   10. Politics, Practical—United States—
Handbooks, manuals, etc.   I. Title.

    F279.B3R38 2004
    975.7'99—dc22

                                                                      2003019473

Designed by Gretchen Achilles

www.fsgbooks.com

10   9   8   7   6   5   4   3   2   1

To the people of Beaufort

who with great grace took us in;

and in particular

To Henry, Liza, Lily, and Jack—

together forever through thick and thin.

Contents

Preface   ix

PART ONE
Gaining Power
    1. Do Something   3
    2. Show Your Teeth   19
    3. Constituencies   24
    4. Open Seats   30
    5. Coming from Behind   34
    6. Friends   37
    7. Money   47
    8. Campaign Bumps   59
    9. Going Negative   64

PART TWO
Holding Power
   10. Symbols   71
   11. Getting Started   74
   12. Clear the Table   80
   13. Find the Capitals   91
   14. Illusion   96
   15. Principle   112
   16. Getting Results   133
   17. The Direct Threat   139

18. The Indirect Threat   142
19. Mean It   155
20. Leaking   162
21. Spinning   169
22. Creating Cover   176
23. Counterpunching   186
24. Taking Credit   192
25. Dancing with the Wolves   201

PART THREE

Losing Power

26. Scandal   209
27. Running from Behind   215
28. Elder Statesman   218
29. Coming Back   224

Preface

THE Beaufort County, South Carolina, Board of Elections uses for its offices a maze of tiny workspaces crammed into a former classroom halfway down the hall of a dismal one-story school building. The ceilings in the place are stained from roof leaks. The board uses a schoolroom down the hall for its conference room: blackboards, fluorescent lights and all.

It is to this most unlikely of places that up until last year candidates came on election nights to watch election workers write the results of the day's voting on the blackboards. Those nights the conference room was jammed with office-seekers, TV camera crews, reporters, lawyers, political junkies, nuts off the street, and other friends and supporters of various descriptions.

All the candidates for all the offices in Beaufort County threw themselves into this election-night skinny-dip every four years.

If you wanted to be sure to look your worst on television and be quoted in newspapers saying the stupidest of things, then you jumped on in too. This is the way it was always done in Beaufort, the county seat of Beaufort County, the fastest-growing county in South Carolina. I am privileged to serve as Beaufort's mayor, so I have seen the skinny-dip first hand.

But I have never jumped into it, and I may as well say why right up front.

I was lucky in the years shortly after I completed my schooling. By a series of coincidences and a lot of long days as an itinerant journalist in northern Michigan, in Greenwich Village, in Boston, and then on Long Island, I ended up in city hall in New York City in 1978 working as the advance man for Mayor Ed Koch. I was twenty-seven years old and I was paid $13,500 a year.

Mayor John Lindsay had a dozen or so advance men. Facing the fiscal crisis in 1975, Mayor Abraham Beame cut the force to four. Then came Ed Koch and the second fiscal crisis. For all of Ed's first term I was his only advance man. Everywhere Ed went for those four years I went there first to scope out the room and the crowd. It was before cell phones. They gave me a black city-owned Plymouth Matador with year-round snow tires and an unmarked police car package, and an NYPD walkie-talkie that connected to the mayor's car. I brought my own cheap suit.

Ed's trademark was the quick in-and-out: getting in, going right to the microphone, speaking just long enough to grab a headline, and then begging off for the next event. He went everywhere . . . for fifteen minutes. He was saving the greatest city in the world.

And I got there first, usually having screamed there under lights and sirens.

After Ed won reelection in 1981 with 76 percent of the vote, he decided to run for governor of the state of New York the following year. My job was to be the campaign controller and the chief advance man. We lost to Mario Cuomo in the primary. Mario went on to win the general too. Ed wasn't at his best in that campaign. In his mind, although he never told me this, the calculation was a choice between two unspeakable evils for him: living upstate or having Mario Cuomo be governor while Ed was mayor. In the very messy 1977 New York mayoral campaign, Ed had defeated Cuomo, whom five years later Ed feared would use his position as governor to exact revenge upon Ed and the city. Ed derives his enormous energy from the city, and Albany, or anywhere else, would have left him flat.

In the months spent campaigning for governor while still serving as the city's mayor, Ed spent just two nights upstate. And they were compulsory: the two nights of the state Democratic convention in Syracuse.

After that campaign we all returned somewhat chastened to city hall, not a bad place to return to if you have wounds to lick. In about the middle of Ed's second term as mayor, his third press secretary left. They were burning out about one every two years. He asked me if I wanted the job and I accepted. I did the job for about four years. During that time Ed and I worked together on two of his books, *Mayor* and *Politics*. *Mayor* appeared in 1983 and was a bestseller. Political observers credited it with restoring to Ed the luster he had lost in the gubernatorial debacle. Whether it did or didn't, Ed overwhelmingly won a third term as mayor in 1985. His opponent in the all-important Democratic primary was City Council President Carol Bellamy. Carol's office was about one hundred yards from Ed's in city hall. In between were his press office, her press office, and Room 9, the legendary bull pen from which the city hall press corps operates. In a set-up like that, especially with two twenty-four-hour news radio stations covering the city, news cycles lasted about half an hour each.

Shortly after Ed was sworn in for his third term, the Bess Myerson "Mess" and Parking Violations Bureau scandals simultaneously engulfed city hall. This was the two-year news story that made the political career of Rudolph Giuliani and caused Queens Borough President Donny Manes to take his own life. As those dark days were concluding, I left city hall for Wall Street. I was thirty-six years old.

I had grown up in city hall. Back home in Indiana none of my family were in public life. What I know about politics I learned from the cast of extraordinary characters who saved New York from bankruptcy in the late '70s and ran it through the highs and lows of the '80s. Ed Koch, of course, but also Dan Wolf, Bobby Wagner, David Garth, Stanley Friedman, John LoCicero, Donny Manes, Maureen Connelly, Stanley Brezenoff, Victor Botnick, Linda Cahill, Ben Ward, Diane Coffey, and Henry Stern—some now dead, some disappeared, some gone on to greater glories, these were the planets in the Koch City Hall universe. All of them contributed to my education, and all of them, like Ed, are practical, results-oriented people.

After a couple of years in mergers and acquisitions, I'd had enough. I took my profits and, with my wife and our infant daughter and two-year-old son, moved to Beaufort, the jewel of the South Carolina lowcountry. We wanted to raise our children in a small town where they'd know everyone and everyone would know them. That was the way it had been for us as kids. She was from Camden in the South Carolina midlands. I was from the outskirts of Indianapolis. We only knew one family in Beaufort, and we didn't know them well. Beaufort was a small town then and it's still a small town. In the fifteen years I've lived in Beaufort the town has grown from about 10,000 to about 13,000, which makes New York about 700 times bigger than Beaufort. We restored the haunted house in town and moved in, and I returned to my first love, newspapering, and started up a weekly, *The Lowcountry Ledger*. I gave it my heart and my soul, but I couldn't make it return a reasonable profit. On a sad day in the bad times of 1992 I folded up the *Ledger*. The next spring the woman who ran the Historic Beaufort Foundation, Cynthia Cole, sat me down and asked me to run for the Beaufort City Council. The announced candidates were all Good Ole Boys, she said, and it wouldn't matter which one won because they'd all be awful.

I decided to make a run for it. I ran a practical, results-oriented campaign with a simple message and ended up the top vote-getter.

All elected officials need to get their messages across, but there is one group to which constituent communication is all important: the outsider. That was me: the Yankee running in the city where 130 years before the Articles of Secession were drafted. It is to this group—political outsiders—that this book is addressed.

In every town there is an establishment, an existing power structure, and most often in most towns public officials represent the interests of this establishment. Often elected officials' financial interests are inextricably intertwined with the financial interests of the town's power structure. There is nothing necessarily wrong with that. It is, in fact, the norm. It is, moreover, the way a representative democracy was first envisioned, at least by Alexander Hamilton and the Federalists. These establishment-elected officials have generally worked their way up through civic clubs and various public committees. They know the reporters and the way the game is played, or at least they have easy access to those who do.

Occasionally, however, an individual comes along who wants to challenge the power structure, who is willing to try to live by his or her political wits outside the cozy confines of the establishment. She may be a housewife who gets steamed up about the siting of a school and decides to do something about the city's dumb zoning laws. He may be a retired history teacher who goes to a meeting and is appalled by some selectman's rudeness, and decides to run to bring civility to his local government. Or he may be the owner of the tree service in town who decides the city isn't treating its trees well enough, so he runs for city council. These candidates often bring with them a simple, selfless agenda: they seek to improve the city's quality of life for their constituents.

Our localities need more of these. They bring with them fresh ideas and more often than not, they move their towns and cities ahead in surprising and refreshing ways. However, for these elected officials, hard-wired communication with the constituency is essential. It is political life or death. Because they are outsiders, they are often not politically savvy when they arrive in office. Some may never have been interviewed by a reporter before they got into the controversy that launched them into public life.

It is to these change agents, who want to make their towns better just because they can be better, that this book is directed.

The election nights in New York in the elections of 1981, 1982, and 1985 ran in a very different way from the classroom in Beaufort. Here's how: Each campaign rented a suite in one of the large midtown hotels, and the candidate and his or her staffers and family went there to await the results. Each campaign also rented a ballroom in the same hotel. There the campaign's press people set up all the risers and mult boxes and klieg lights and electronic paraphernalia that will make it possible for the candidate to look and sound best for the cameras. During the course of that very long day, Ed Koch, at least, and his speechwriter got together on two speeches, one for a loss and one for a win. He carried both in his coat pocket. Once the results were known the losing candidate called the winner to concede. There was some jockeying to the concession part because there's always a race for the live shot at the top of the eleven o'clock news. Once the concession calls were completed, first the loser and then the winner went down to their respective ballrooms to make their statements.

In Beaufort you don't have to go to the expense of renting ballrooms and suites. In fact, in most municipal or countywide races that would be silly. But the schoolroom was no alternative either. It makes no sense to me to have TV cameras in your face when you first hear whether you've won or lost. Surely common sense dictates that you be able to take a few minutes to collect your thoughts before facing the cameras. There must be something in between.

There is, of course: stay home. That's what I do, and it works just fine. Invite your friends and supporters over. Send a trusted lawyer over to the schoolroom in case your campaign needs to be represented at a manual recount. Tell the reporters in advance where you'll be and what the phone number there is. Once the results are known, go to a quiet room for a moment, pull out the notes you made for your winning and losing speeches. Collect your thoughts. Write a couple of lines down on an index card.

Win or lose, go easy on the booze.

If you lose, the TV camera crews may or may not want to find you and the chances are you will wish not to have been found anyway.

If you win, the TV camera crews will find you and you can talk to them on your terms in a place where you feel comfortable. Find a place in your house that is bright and where the background looks homey. You'll look a lot better at home, and be more relaxed and cogent, than you will speaking off the cuff under the fluorescent lights back at the schoolroom.

Talk to the cameras one at a time. Take the least important one first, if you can, so that you can practice your statement. If you have children, involve them in the victory celebration. There is no harm at all and a great deal more charm in claiming your victory in your own home with your children in their pajamas. It is their victory too.

Your appearance on camera is a consideration, but finding a way to be sure you know what you want to say and how you want to say it is the main thing. Television producers may like the convenience of having all the candidates in one room and the *cinema verité* feel of the camera stuck in a candidate's face. But the candidate has no obligation to play their game.

That is what this book is: practical, results-oriented political methods learned in New York's city hall and applied in Beaufort, or in towns and small cities everywhere. It is not about the right or wrong policies by which cities and towns in the twenty-first century should be run. Yes, I have views on these things, lots of them, but when I share them in the following pages it is only because they help to illustrate one of the ways of getting your message across. This book is about the ways. It is not about the messages. In the early chapters I will seek to catalog the skills and techniques with which first-time candidates for local office should become familiar. In the middle chapters I will direct the reader's attention particularly to the ways power can be efficiently used to affect change. And in the final few chapters I'll devote my attentions to the ways effective elected officials conduct themselves in the final phases of their careers.

Most of what's here will sound like common sense. It is. But believe me it's been learned the hard way. If for a moment the narrator, me, begins to sound like the hero of this book, I ask the reader to recall that it is the nature of political diarists to portray their own cups as half full.

JANUARY 4, 2004

Beaufort, South Carolina

PART ONE

Gaining Power

1. Do Something

TO win a seat in your local government it is helpful to have distinguished yourself by doing something that a significant sector of the electorate wanted to see done. If getting that good thing accomplished means you consorted with radicals on the fringe, that's not a problem. But before the race goes off, you should demonstrate your responsible nature by moving into the mainstream.

Across America there are parks and hospitals that need building and shopping centers in the middle of nowhere and expressways through neighborhoods that need stopping. There are also many badly needed libraries, schools, paths, roads, and bridges. Spearhead one of those efforts successfully and you have taken a big first step.

Americans like their representatives to be tough fighters. It makes sense. When you get elected you have been chosen to represent a group of otherwise essentially powerless individuals against a potentially all-powerful government. You are their defender, one of their very few. While it can be good to be smart, if you can be only one thing, it's better to be a relentless advocate for your constituents, individually and as a group. There are plenty of smart folks in the political boneyard who spent their time being smart and not helping their constituents.

It's a plus to look good. It's a plus to speak well. It's a plus to know at least one of the issues in depth. But it is essential that you be perceived as tough. If you get knocked down, get up, brush yourself off with grace, stay in touch with your friends, wait quietly for the next election cycle, and come out swinging. The chances are you'll be stronger than you were before.

One of the most beautiful two-lane country roads in America runs seventeen miles south and east from Beaufort, South Carolina, across several of the Sea Islands, and out to the Atlantic Ocean. As it sets out from Beaufort, U.S. 21, as it is known, crosses an exquisite 1959 erector-set-style swing-span bridge over the Atlantic Intracoastal Waterway. From there, as it leaves the complexities of the city behind, the road meanders past saltwater marshes and along tidal creeks as it approaches a number of historic places. Crossing over Chowan Creek and its savannahs, at mile five the road passes on to St. Helena Island, the center of America's Gullah culture, where for hundreds of years people of West African descent have adapted their old world culture to the new world ways of the Anglo-Saxon Christians.

On our left a few more miles along is a two-story corner store that was the commercial hub of the Sea Island cotton boom from 1830 through the 1850s, and across the road is a one-story loft that was the island's first African-American co-op after the War of Northern Aggression, as it is sometimes called in these parts.

From that historic crossroads, U.S. 21 passes a giant live oak tree, known locally as the Emancipation Oak, in whose shade 135 years ago the slaves of the planters were gathered to hear the Emancipation Proclamation read for the first time. Then the road runs back out into the country—and back into time—and motorists are treated to the sight of grazing cattle with glimpses of the St. Helena Sound in the distance. At about mile twelve the road rounds a wide bend and reveals a mile-long savannah, passes a shrimpers' dock, crosses another swing-span bridge, and meanders among small inland islands and the barrier islands that mark the Atlantic, until at mile seventeen it ends at the gates of privately owned Fripp Island.

Early in 1991 the South Carolina Highway Commission announced that it would widen to five lanes the section of U.S. 21 that runs from Beaufort onto St. Helena Island, past the corner store and the Emancipation Oak. The Commission also declared that when funding was available they intended to make the road five lanes all the way to the beaches.

The tiny environmental community in Beaufort County knew that real estate development follows government-funded infrastructure improvements. Put another way, big housing developments don't get built where there aren't highways and where there isn't access to a sewage treatment facility.

The U.S. 21 corridor was already zoned for commercial development. Sanitary sewer access was already on parts of St. Helena Island. All that was missing was the highway. With the highway would come the housing developments, the Zippy Lubes and Burger Kings and drive-thru banks and dry cleaners that are such familiar fixtures on the outskirts of post–World War II American cities. When the Highway Commission widens that road, the environmentalists said to one another, St. Helena is finished.

There is a natural reluctance among those who have been around government for a while to step in the way of "progress." I had been around government for a while, and so I was reluctant. Moreover, I was a newcomer, having just moved into Beaufort's historic district three years earlier. The South Carolina Highway Commission had never been beaten. The local elected officials were lined up behind the project. The Good Ole Boys who are the establishment in small southern towns and who stood to benefit from the public investment were vigorously—even jubilantly—behind the elected officials. Here was big government finally poised to make a big investment in a place that a generation before had been the poorest place in the poorest state in the United States.

As a newspaperman by training, I knew there were two sides to the story. But as a husband and father and new citizen of my newly adopted hometown, I couldn't stand to think of this beautiful road turned over time into just another suburban-anywhere streetscape. The beauty of the road was just the beginning. Development would inevitably drive up land prices and taxes, and the escalation would change the whole area. Poor people whose families received their land from the Lincoln Administration would be forced off it after 130 years. Farmers would quit farming and try to become developers of their crop land, at least until they discovered the vast sums that must be amassed to push large developments forward. Then they would simply sell out to the big boys from Atlanta. A beautiful and unique place was about to lose its character. As someone who wanted to see my new hometown thrive, there was a further consideration: the widened road would inevitably draw economic vitality out of the city.

The *Ledger* covered the story, but to me it just wasn't enough. While a newspaper can sound the alarm, activists must answer it. But they didn't. My first call was to Dana Beach, a founder of the South Carolina Coastal Conservation League, based in Charleston, seventy-five miles north of Beaufort. Not only are these people the best environmental group in South Carolina, they are the best at what they do of any group between the Chesapeake Bay and Miami. But as a group they were only three years old, and had never gotten involved in Beaufort County politics. Beach was reluctant, but he came down to Beaufort and we sat in my living room and cooked up a strategy that did not involve him in its initial stage.

In the same way that in an election you can't beat somebody with nobody, in a public policy controversy you can't stop a project without a viable alternative. And even then it's a long shot. Sometimes, however, you can get the proposal changed. That was the direction we took.

Viewed most broadly, there were three parts of U.S. 21. There was the part in the city: a city street running through the heart of the city. There was the part the Commission proposed to widen, from the swing-span bridge across Lady's and St. Helena Islands to the Emancipation Oak. And there was the part from the tree to the beach. We focused on the seven-and-a-half-mile middle part from the bridge to the Oak. We decided if we could draw a line in the sand, so to speak, and say "no widening on St. Helena," then we could stop the widening of not only the several miles of the proposed widened road that crossed St. Helena Island, but also all of the future project to widen the road from the Oak to the beach.

At the same time, we focused on the U.S. 21 city street that runs through Beaufort. On the other side of the city, as U.S. 21 comes in from the west, the street is a five-lane strip mall. As it approaches the city's national landmark historic district, however, the road regains its scale, that of a four-lane boulevard, and as it enters the district it narrows to two lanes, changes its name to Carteret Street, and sweeps around a dramatic ninety-degree turn at the edge of the Beaufort River before proceeding past the college, and out toward the islands.

A quaint city street with a five-lane highway on either end is a recipe for disaster: a one-mile bottleneck in the middle of a thirty-five-mile-long five-lane expressway. Moreover, were it to be widened into an expressway, it would run highway traffic through, and thus divide, the city's historic district, the source of much of Beaufort's charm and much of its livelihood. If we could call attention to the threat posed to the historic district, Dana and I reasoned, we could begin to mobilize public opinion against the project. Carteret Street had many more friends in high places than did the stretch of the road out closer to the ocean. Suddenly the residents of the historic district would see the widening as a threat to their tranquil neighborhood, and their property values. Once enlisted to "Save Carteret Street," we hoped they would keep marching on behalf of keeping U.S. 21 a two-lane road out to the islands.

A grassroots effort like stopping a highway or a shopping center, at its essentials, is just like getting a bill passed. The bill's advocates try to tailor the bill to benefit as many constituent groups as possible. This is what lobbyists get paid millions of dollars to do every year in Washington. The money gets paid because the benefits to various business groups are so great, and because the terrain is relatively complicated. But basic "consensus building" work is pretty simple, especially at the local level. Only a working knowledge of your community is required. "Who stands to benefit from what we are trying to do?" is the basic question. "If we do it this way, will it benefit so-and-so as well?" "Are we willing to do that to get his, her, their support?" "Who's against us?" "What can we do to temper their opposition?" "Under what circumstances can their group be divided?" Those are the secondary questions.

At that first meeting in my living room, Dana and I determined that two grassroots advocacy groups should be formed:

the Carteret Street Association and the Sea Island Scenic Parkway Coalition. Dana then put me in touch with Ken Driggers at the then two-year-old Palmetto Conservation Foundation in Columbia, which specialized in working side-by-side with neighborhood groups, land trusts, and governments to help them do good planning.

After organizing a handful of my neighbors into the Carteret Street Association, we passed the hat among concerned merchants on Carteret Street. With their $50 and $100 contributions came their unwavering support. We also received larger contributions from individuals who were more affluent and who just loved beauty, many the residents of the antebellum homes in the historic district who had chosen to live in Beaufort for its combination of natural and urban beauty.

Funding the Sea Island Scenic Parkway Coalition's plan promised to be a more difficult proposition. The merchants' group, the Lady's Island Business and Professionals Association, was deeply divided on whether widening U.S. 21 to five lanes was in their financial interest; some of them stood to benefit directly and others feared that opposing the Good Ole Boys might be bad for business.

For their part, the hundred or so African-American families whose community would be divided by the new highway were generally people of enthusiasm, but also of limited means.

How could we get the money to pay Ken Driggers for an alternative plan? Finally we decided we'd try to get the county government to fund it. There was no assurance that if the county ended up favoring a design that was at variance with the highway commission's that the commission would yield to the county.

But that was a problem for a later day.

Now we needed a spark to light a fire under the county council, a Sam Adams to stage a Boston Tea Party. Here was the opportunity for the extremists to play their traditional role.

The best carpenter in Beaufort is a guy named Howard Mills. Howie sailed into town on his cutter, *The Bear*, in 1988, and stayed, never once cutting off his beard and ponytail. He is so good with wood that he can pick his jobs and write his own ticket, both of which he does with thorough independence. He grew up in San Diego, so he had seen the future and he knew it wasn't pretty. Moreover, Howie lived on St. Helena Island, so he rode U.S. 21 virtually every day.

Shortly before the county council was to consider the matter, Howie hit upon a simple scheme. He got a roll of orange plastic surveyor's marking tape, and late one night he drove along a particularly fragile portion of the highway and marked every huge live oak tree within a hundred yards. After wrapping tape around perhaps a dozen majestic oak trees, he drove home.

The next morning the marked trees were the talk of Beaufort. People said they "had no idea the road was going to be so big, that so many live oaks would have to come down." It was, of course, assumed that the highway commission's surveyors had put up the markings. That afternoon, when questioned by a reporter, the commission's spokesman denied their having had anything to do with it; and once he'd denied their involvement, the commission couldn't very well send crews out to take the ribbons down. So the orange ribbons stayed and the line in the sand was drawn. The County Council said they'd fund the Palmetto Conservation Foundation's study. Our plan would become their plan.

Now we waited, it seemed forever.

The Carteret Street Association's plan was completed first. It called for historic-looking streetlamps, new brick crosswalks, and young trees, all of which would have to be torn up if the road were widened.

Up in Columbia the highway commission was miffed that the county council had hired an independent consultant to second-guess them. The highway commissioner who represented Beaufort was a neighbor of mine in Beaufort, former lieutenant governor W. Brantley Harvey. Brantley, as he is known throughout Beaufort, is the son of a prominent politician, and he was also one of the two lead partners in the biggest law firm in Beaufort. A true son of the South, he is a wonderfully articulate genteel Southern gentleman, with a fiery tenseness evident just below the surface.

At the time—things have changed—Brantley, in effect, ran the department for the seven-county district he represented on the commission, and he was determined to five-lane U.S. 21 out to the ocean.

Small towns being what they are, I began receiving phone calls from strangers, who would recite what they knew of Brantley's real estate interests along U.S. 21. His plan, as they described it to me, was classic Good Ole Boy stuff. The former lieutenant governor and big lawyer in town gets a political appointment to the highway commission, and then reshuffles the deck of improvements so that the one on top happens to be the one that will improve his own property. That's what they told me. I never knew whether it was true. Those who went to look at the deeds found the properties owned by limited liability corporations with nondescript names.

Ken Driggers cajoled traffic count information out of the highway department and hired a traffic engineer to analyze the data. He held several public informational meetings, all raucous affairs. He solicited comments from all the local governments.

And he met privately with many of the local elected officials. After all that, he unveiled the county's plan: three-lane sections in shopping areas, some four-lane divided parkway sections out in the country, and some intersection improvements in the two-lane sections—particularly on St. Helena Island. With the county's draft plan in hand he embarked on another round of raucous meetings.

The pro-development interests were often but by no means exclusively represented by Red Mitchell, who owned the Texaco filling station and convenience store across the street from the 1830s two-story store. Red got his name either from his red hair or because of the way his face flushes when he becomes agitated. Red's family were tomato farmers, but as the county grew they had gone into building and land development, and now owned some large undeveloped tracts. Red, then in his forties, was in touch with many of the landowners along the corridor, and their position was clear: "There's going to be progress and development on Lady's and St. Helena Islands. People have invested their money here. We don't want to infringe on anyone else's rights, and we don't want anyone infringing on ours. We have waited long enough for this road. Let's not turn it down and have the money go to some other county's road project. This is our tax money, finally a little of it coming back home to benefit us. The development has begun. The government has encouraged it. You can't stop it. If the government tries to limit our rights to improve our land, it's a 'taking' and the government will never get out of court alive."

Arguing for cultural preservation were a half dozen African-American community leaders, but let me characterize Ernestine Atkins as the spokesperson for the group. Ernestine grew up in what is known around Beaufort as a family compound: five houses sprinkled between oaks and palmetto trees and lined up along the mile-wide St. Helena Sound on twenty of the most pristine acres in America. Ernestine is a diminutive, soft-spoken, and immensely cheerful but resolute lady in her fifties. To put food on the table, she runs a literacy program in which she goes into the homes of illiterate families and reads to the parents and children.

Ernestine Atkins's position was as follows: "Eustis is our community. This is where we grew up. Eustis is where our fathers and their fathers grew up. It is, God willing, where our children and their children will grow up too. But it is a fragile place and an expressway with fast food businesses strung along it will change the way we live forever. Our children won't be able to cross the new road. Lady's Island will be divided, and that will be the end of Eustis as the community it is and has been."

Taking a third, the environmentalist, position would be Elayne Scott, who ran an art gallery on the ground floor of the 1830s building, where she liked to host fundraisers for liberal causes such as the admission of women to the Citadel. An effusive personality, Elayne opposes on principle, for examples, all billboards, tree-cutting, and asphalt on St. Helena and elsewhere. Her position was this: "The Eustis Community and St. Helena Island are national treasures and great places to live. Crabs and shrimp swim freely in our waters. We can pick oysters and bring them home to our tables. People know one another. They help one another. Don't destroy all that we enjoy together so that a few can make some money. How much do they need? Tell us, we'll pass the hat."

As the controversy crept into its second year, the interest groups got better organized and dug in deeper. There was no easy way for the county council to duck the issues, yet it still wasn't clear there would be any muscle to their final recommendation, whatever it would be.

In all controversies there is a seminal moment: a meeting where excessive hypocrisy or greed is displayed, or a demonstration where moderate people behave immoderately. These are the moments that turn around crowds, and public opinion, and elected officials.

In September 1992 the county held a public meeting in the Lady's Island Middle School's auditorium to explain the two plans and their decision-making process. Those of us who opposed the widening decided it was time we played every card in our hand. So we made up a petition addressed to the South Carolina Ethics Commission calling for an investigation of Commissioner Harvey's dual role as highway commissioner and landowner of two tracts along U.S. 21. (Because of the blind corporations, we didn't even know for sure that he had an interest in the land.) We couldn't find anyone courageous enough to pass the petition, so we just left a dozen or so copies of it on a table outside the auditorium, hoping that a few courageous folks might sign it.

Several hundred people from all sides of the issue showed up for the meeting. On his way into the auditorium, Commissioner Harvey read the petition and very shrewdly picked up the whole stack and put them in his briefcase. But he couldn't be sure he had them all, and the accusation made him angry. It is never good in public life to become angry, especially when you are about to address hundreds of people. While it is sometimes beneficial to appear to be shocked or outraged, it is a big mistake to let actual anger, which is self-indulgent, overwhelm your tactical savvy.

When it came his turn to speak, Brantley launched, in obvious anger, into a defense of himself and the merits of the widening. In an enormous public relations blunder, he concluded by denying any wrongdoing. While the matter had been whispered about for a year, no one had said anything publicly. No one had the guts. And they probably weren't going to get them. So most of the people in the room were hearing about Brantley's purported conflict for the first time, and from the accused man himself. It was Nixon's "I am not a crook" line, and it played just as poorly.

Commissioner Harvey's public defense of himself became the lead of the reporters' stories the next day. The meeting became the seminal moment. As the commissioner sought to recover over the following weeks, he became uncharacteristically conciliatory, saying, in effect, "I believe the road should be widened to five lanes all the way out to the beach. If we don't do it now we'll regret it later. People will die because the ambulances and fire trucks couldn't get through the traffic. But I understand there is not unanimity on the design and so, as your highway commissioner, I'll support whatever recommendation the county council makes."

It was the right thing to say, and to this day I applaud Brantley for saying it. It also broke new ground in South Carolina, where highway commissioners had up until then been judge and jury of the merits of the highway projects proposed for their districts.

The county council was thus empowered to make the final call. And so we turned our attentions upon them as they grappled with the daunting task of designing a controversial highway by committee in open session.

Our position was unchanged, and we lobbied aggressively for it: no widening on St. Helena Island except the improvement of a handful of intersections.

In meetings with another of my neighbors, Beth Grace, the county council vice chairman who represented the Beaufort City district, we set our strategies and sought to line up the votes. Some council members were committed one way or another, but the swing votes were waiting to hear the debate. When we saw that we'd have to pick up some of the votes in the room, we knew what we had to do.

Nina Morais worked on St. Helena Island doing community preservation work. She knew the preachers and the deacons and the members of the auxiliaries and boards of elders at the churches there. Nina, a tireless organizer, was dead set against the wider road, and she made it her mission to make sure that whenever the county council met to discuss the road, the room would be packed with the church-going ladies and gentlemen of St. Helena Island.

Nina went down to the print shop and got one thousand small yellow bumper stickers printed up: "No 5 Lanes on St. Helena." Some people put them on their cars, but they were really for the meetings. As soon as Beth let me know when and where the next council meeting would be, I called Nina. Nina called the pastors and arranged for the church buses to convey the ladies and gentlemen there. When each bus pulled into the government parking lot, Nina would step aboard, give a little speech of thanks, and pass out her stickers. Then the ladies and gentlemen would affix the stickers prominently to their clothing, and file silently into the meeting room. To my knowledge, none of them ever said a single public word. They simply filed in, listened politely, and filed out. But the outcome could not have been the same without their powerful presence.

After two years of struggle, Council in a series of votes finally expressed its will. There would be no five lanes on St. Helena Island, and the rest of the project was scaled down to manageable proportions.

The highway commission had been defeated. And something else had happened. The people of Beaufort County had begun to perceive that life was changing in our part of the world. Once the poorest county in South Carolina, ours was now the richest. They began to openly wonder whether all growth was good growth. A huge housing development twenty miles away, Sun City Hilton Head, would soon act as a catalyst for supercharged growth for that part of the county. Together, the U.S. 21 controversy in the northern part of the county and the introduction of Sun City to the south were a wake-up call. If the present residents wanted to preserve their genteel and personal way of life, they now knew they would have to take a role in their local government.

Why do I tell this story? Because the best way to get ready for your first campaign is by getting something done before you run. Getting something done requires working with others. This is where your political supporters will come from. I hadn't known that at the time, and my involvement in the road widening issue had nothing to do with some imagined future run for political office. At the time I would have told you I couldn't be elected.

But five years later, when I ran for mayor, Beth Grace wrote a key letter endorsing my candidacy, and her daughter Katherine worked in my campaign day-to-day. Ernestine Atkins told her friends in the city's African-American community that they could trust me. Nina Morais helped draft letters to the editor for people who wanted to say nice things about me, but who were self-conscious about their writing abilities. The Carteret Street merchants gave me campaign contributions and talked up my candidacy. The historic preservation community knew me and trusted me and supported me with their checkbooks. These people became my core supporters—because we had come from somewhere together.

2. Show Your Teeth

POLITICIANS don't take seriously those people who can't hurt them. To win a local race you must demonstrate that you are "a player." In trucker jargon, to get off the porch you will need to show that you are one of the big dogs.

There are several ways to do this. You can roil up a community and lead them as their spokesperson into city hall. You can walk off Air Force One with the president. You can write a big check and get the arts center at the local university named after you. Or you can blow up somebody's well-laid plans by planting an attack story. The Air Force One ride is the most fun. But the attack story costs the least in time and money.

When it comes time to throw a government process off the track, the well-placed news story is the best way to begin. It is absolutely amazing how even just one well-placed story can change the dynamics of a decision. But getting that story isn't automatic. In fact, getting turnaround stories is what public relations consultants get paid lots of money to know how to do. Here's how they do it.

A year or so before I ran for city council, a controversy arose in Beaufort around the installation of a satellite dish. A brokerage house, Edward D. Jones, had applied for a city building permit to put a large dish on the roof of a building they had just leased in the historic district. They said they needed the dish to get stock quotes instantly and to offer video conference sessions with analysts for their customers. They also said they had an FCC permit for the dish. The City of Beaufort building permit was tripping along through the process when I got involved.

The preservationists in Beaufort were concerned. They said the dish on the roof was inappropriate in the historic district and in violation of the secretary of the interior's guidelines for best management practices in historic districts.

Cynthia Cole, who was the executive director of the Historic Beaufort Foundation (HBF), called me up. She was exercised about the dish and wanted to know if I knew anything about how the FCC works and whether it could trump the interior department.

I said that sounded to me like the kind of problem that would end up in either the federal courts or the White House or both, and before anything got sorted out at either place the dish would have been sitting on Edward D. Jones's roof for several years.

"How about a little adverse publicity for Edward D. Jones?" I proffered. "If they're trying to sell stocks to rich people in Beaufort, I'll bet they don't want to get sideways with the preservation community. Let's see how tough they are."

"What do you have in mind?" Cindy, who is a natural-born street-fighter dressed up like a Southern lady, asked.

"How about a protest march?" I suggested. "A little street theater?"

In Beaufort at that time the only place that had ever been protested against on the sidewalk was the local abortion clinic, which had been picketed by the local right-to-life group. Those protests occurred at least once a week, and people were so accustomed to them they didn't even see them any more. So a protest march was a novelty.

Cindy loved the idea and, with some of her HBF volunteer lieutenants, she set out to organize the demonstration. They had to go down to City Hall to get a permit to protest (a local law that was clearly unconstitutional and that has since been repealed), and that set off all kinds of alarms in the building permits department, effectively in itself stalling the dish permit for a couple of weeks.

As the excitement grew about the upcoming "Dump the Dish" protest march, it occurred to me that *The Wall Street Journal* might be interested in the story. My thinking was if *The Beaufort Gazette* covers the march, which they surely will, it will create some pressure on Edward D. Jones. But if *The Wall Street Journal* covers the march, and the guys at Edward D. Jones's headquarters, who are getting paid to worry about the company's earnings and image, have to concern themselves with what's going on down at the new Beaufort office, the guys in Beaufort will either fold or be ordered by headquarters to fold.

I didn't know anybody at the *Journal*'s home office, but I was a reader and I knew the paper. One of my favorite columns, and one of every reader's favorite columns, is the center column on the front page that focuses on some flaky business success or failure in some far-flung place. I thought that would be the place for this story. So I called around the *Journal*'s offices in New York until I found the editor of that column. Then I pitched her the story.

Most reporters, even business reporters, are sympathetic to preservation and environmental issues. They know their readers like to read about environmental and preservation issues. And if

there's a conflict between a large corporation and an environmental or preservation group, that's news, especially at *The Wall
Street Journal*.

Editors, for their part, love obscure tips. Most of them used
to be reporters and they long for the adventure of the street.
Typically they sit in their offices all day, except when they go out
to lunch, and so they are sensitive about being disconnected. By
passing along a tip to a reporter, the editor conveys to the reporter that the editor isn't disconnected from the real world.

If you're planting a story, there's nothing wrong with calling
an editor. Leaking's different, but we'll get to that.

The editor and I chatted about what was going on for about
ten minutes and she loved the story and she did in fact send a
reporter down to cover the march.

The march was a lark. My friend George Post wrote a protest
song. Others made placards. People wore funny hats with
grotesque-looking satellite dishes taped on them. The thing felt
like a Ban the Bomb march from 1962, except less beatnik and
more country club. It was very "preservation." It lasted about
forty-five minutes.

But the guys at headquarters whose job it was to protect
Jones's stock price failed to see the humor. You could just hear
the CEO getting razzed by his buddies at the Country Club about
how those little old ladies in tennis shoes down in the bayous of
South Carolina were giving him trouble.

The local guys pulled their permit application the next day.
They broke their lease and moved their office and their satellite
dish out of the historic district to a street corner nearby, where, I
am happy to report, they are thriving today.

Marshall McLuhan asked the question, "If a tree falls in the
woods and no one sees it, did it really fall?" Ask yourself, "If a

protest march marches and no one sees it, did the marchers really march?"

The impact of newspaper stories is directly related to their placement within the paper. Newspapers prefer to put "exclusives" on their front pages, when they can. To get the best placement for your story it's therefore first necessary for you to choose the newspaper that the people involved in the decision-making read and are influenced by. On Capitol Hill, that's *The Washington Post*. In Los Angeles it's the *Los Angeles Times*. In New York, at least for the business and political communities, it's *The New York Times*. On Wall Street it's *The Wall Street Journal*. In your hometown it's probably the hometown daily.

Once you've decided where you want your story to appear, call up the reporter you've decided should write the story and tell her she's got the story exclusively, provided it's published within the next seventy-two hours, or whatever time period is reasonable. If you don't know any of the reporters, call or go see the assignments editor. Do not call the paper's editor in chief. That person is probably one of the establishment you're trying to jostle.

Newspaper stories draw their life from controversy. So when pitching a story, make sure to recount what one side says and what the other side says. Then, to be sure to get your best arguments in, explain why your side's right and the other side's wrong. Speak slowly and pause between sentences. Most reporters don't take shorthand.

After the story appears, here's what will happen, although it may be almost imperceptible at first. Because there are no secrets in either small towns or big cities, the politicians will all mysteriously know it was you who planted the attack story. And then you will begin to get respect.

3. Constituencies

IN New York, where mass is said in thirty-three different languages every day, a great deal is made of "ethnic politics." These are the efforts made by office-seekers to find ways to appeal to various ethnic groups. These appeals are made in a variety of ways.

Office-seekers solicit support by visiting the religious leaders of each group. While they are there they talk about how that rebbe or archbishop, for example, will most easily be able to stay in touch with the office-holder's office. This means jobs. In some cases office-holders hire a member of a particularly powerful group to function as a liaison between the group and his office. More often the same result is achieved more subtly. A close look at the personal staffs of savvy governmental officials in New York and in other ethnically diverse cities will reveal they are generally ethnically diverse and more or less reflective of the ethnicity of the city. The ethnic diversity of these office staffs is constructed carefully so that as many powerful individuals in the community as is possible will feel they have "one of their own" as a contact person in city hall.

Savvy office-seekers also march in the annual parades of as many ethnic groups as they can. They get their pictures taken eating the food of each group, and their public relations people make sure those pictures get used in the appropriate ethnic newspapers. They also give interviews to those papers, and in those interviews they take care to demonstrate their understanding of the individual needs of each group. It is more efficient to win the allegiance of a group this way than it is to try to gain with handshakes the votes one by one. It's like buying in bulk.

The same principles of representative government apply in less ethnically diverse cities, towns, and villages.

People naturally live near people like themselves. In New York City the Greeks live in Astoria, the Indians live in Flushing, and the Italians live in Bensonhurst. So if a savvy politician wants to curry favor with Italian Americans, for example, he leads the drive to open a swimming pool or he gets a new firehouse for Bensonhurst.

Where constituencies cannot be readily defined by ethnicity, they can be defined by neighborhoods. Neighborhoods have characteristics individual to themselves. Some of a neighborhood's characteristics are the areas of similarity of the majority of the residents of the neighborhood. Are there lots of descendants of Scandinavian immigrants there? Are there teachers and firemen? Are most of the residents farm workers? Are there many members of labor unions there? Are the residents of the neighborhood largely retired? Or are they mostly starter-home couples? Are there children in strollers there? Are the people college grads? Are they largely affiliated with one or another political party? Is there anyone at home during the working hours?

When you understand a neighborhood in your town well enough to answer questions like these, you have begun to understand one of your constituencies.

The next set of neighborhood questions are questions like these: Do the people who live in this neighborhood want lower taxes? Or would they prefer more services? Do they by and large feel the services they receive are being adequately delivered? Do they want a park? Do they want walking trails? Do they want a grocery store? Or an office park? Is crime too high? Are the water mains corroded? Is traffic congestion getting to be intolerable?

The answers to these questions will tell you what you should be saying to the residents of that neighborhood. You may say to them you have heard the neighborhood ask for more police. You may say the neighborhood is right to want more cops. You may say crime is too high. You may not say, unless you are absolutely certain you can deliver it, that you will see to it that there are additional police patrols in the neighborhood, should you be elected. You don't have to make campaign promises to get elected. You do have to hear each neighborhood and acknowledge to each neighborhood that you have heard them.

It is far better if you have already actually helped.

In 1997 Beaufort County was about to close a county-operated public swimming pool on Green Street, a predominately African-American neighborhood in Beaufort. The county council member who then represented nearly all of the City of Beaufort on the county council, Beth Grace, saw the county staff's recommendation in her agenda packet on a Friday. The matter was scheduled to be debated and voted on Monday.

She called me. I was shocked. There had been no notice. It was a sneak attack.

There is an AM radio station in Beaufort, WVGB, whose listeners are predominantly African American. Jabari Moketsu has a talk show on Saturday mornings. I showed up at the station and asked to go on the show. Jabari asked me what was happening, and I explained that there would be a vote at the county council on Monday to close the pool and replace it with a new one at a school in a white neighborhood a couple of miles away. I said I'd be going to the hearing to urge the council not to take their staff's recommendation and to build the new pool at the same recreational complex where the old, deteriorating one was. I urged his listeners to come on down to the hearing, and bring a friend.

The hearing was packed, and the speakers spoke with passion about the importance of the pool to their neighborhood. County Council couldn't take the pressure, and they folded right there.

When I ran for mayor three years later, that incident was cited repeatedly by my supporters in the African-American community as proof that I could be trusted. Saving the Green Street Pool was a neighborhood issue, but it was ethnic politics too.

You build these blocks one at a time. But in the end you have a citadel.

In 1999, while the mayoral campaign was going on, a separate measure on the ballot asked the city voters whether the city ought to sell the city's water and sewer system to the Beaufort-Jasper Water and Sewer Authority, the regional provider. Sewage treatment was getting very expensive in this fragile place at that time, and the plant needed millions of dollars worth of work that the city couldn't even come close to affording. For too many years the city had taken its water profits and used them to pay police officers and for other general fund expenditures. If the city did the needed work now, water bills would go through the roof.

Meanwhile the water authority was in a contest with Beaufort County over who should be the regional provider. The county wanted to edge the authority out. For that reason the authority wanted to grow as fast as it could. Gaining the city's system would give them an advantage in their contest with the county, so the water authority offered us a very good price. They wanted us to be their poster child. That was okay by me. I said I'd vote for the sale. My opponents were split on the issue, so this was a matter that set us apart. And I was on the side of cheap rates.

When the city had built its sewage treatment plant, the plant had been out in the country. But by the time I came on the scene, the ten-acre plant was adjoined by the Mossy Oaks and Waddell Gardens neighborhoods. Depending upon which way the wind was blowing, some days Mossy Oaks stunk like an open sewer; other days it was Waddell Gardens' turn. These are the neighborhoods where many teachers and retired military families live, people who pay their taxes and don't ask for much back from their city.

Because I like to walk neighborhoods and ring doorbells, I had smelled the smell and I had heard the complaints. You learn a lot out there. And you get some doors slammed in your face. To me they are badges of glory. A door in the face means you are somebody who is doing something.

Early in the 1999 campaign, I proposed that the water authority take the plant over, and after it was surplused as it would eventually have to be, that the water authority return it to the city, and that the city could then use the land only as a park. I said I'd demand that the water authority put a "springing covenant" on the deed. The water authority readily agreed because the prospect of one day trading the plant in for a park would help induce voters to vote for the sale. And the water authority wanted the voters to vote "yes" too.

The neighborhood had no park. The people who lived there couldn't believe it when I told them my plan. The men thought about the effect upon their property values when the stink went away. They thought about backyard barbecues in the fresh air. The women thought about strolling their babies between blooming azalea bushes in the new park and about their husbands and sons playing ball there. My proposal was a home run.

When the city council debated the issue, my campaign mailed all the registered voters in that neighborhood the newspaper coverage of the debate. When the resolution was signed by then Mayor David Taub, we mailed all the voters in the neighborhood copies of it. When the springing covenant was filed at the courthouse, we mailed copies of it too.

When the votes were counted, these were the precincts— and they were as far away from my home district as was possible within the city—that voted for me in the greatest numbers.

Look at your town, or district, as a candidate for national office would look at the United States. Ask yourself why someone in each state would vote for you. Ask yourself why someone from each significant ethnic group would vote for you. If there are good reasons, get them on paper and start mailing them to the appropriate registered voters. If there aren't good reasons yet, you've got more work to do.

4. Open Seats

THE old political adage goes "You can't beat some-body with nobody." Yet a lot of nobodies become somebodies every political season. How do they do it?

The first thing nobodies who become somebodies rarely do is run against incumbents. Incumbency brings with it name recognition. It often means there is a record of achievement that inspires a sense in the electorate that they know the work product they can expect from the incumbent. And there is the not-to-be-discounted ability on the part of the incumbent to get onto the TV and radio and into the newspapers virtually at will. Moreover, incumbents have the full power of the government behind them. They can fill potholes, dispatch police officers, get errors in water bills corrected, expedite paperwork processing, fix street lamps, and get vacant lots cleaned up all day long. And when they're good, they do. Finally, incumbents have seniority, and not just in the Washington or state capital sense. Seniority at the local level means knowing all the other politicians and having a record working with them. The people want their governments to get along. So it's important to be perceived as someone who knows the other governmental leaders and who can get along with them in such a way that the people you represent get their fair share.

Reporters also favor incumbents, especially those who have been good at returning the reporters' phone calls. Like everyone else, reporters generally don't like change. Newcomers are "wild cards." Incumbents (especially those who return their calls before deadline) are "old hands."

Early in a political career, a hard run against an incumbent may set the stage for future glory. But no matter what the attributes of the challenger, a run against an incumbent must be regarded as a long shot. Year in and year out, the voters as a group are not the kind of gamblers who play long shots.

A short look at the early careers of a couple of the American democracy's great campaigners and vote-getters is instructive. In 1886, in his first try for elective office, Teddy Roosevelt, a gifted speaker and tireless campaigner, ran last in a three-way race for mayor of New York City. The voters didn't know who TR was. A little muckraking in Albany; the sudden, unrelated natural deaths on the same day of both his wife and mother; a couple of years as the city's new broom police commissioner; a new wife; and stints in Washington in the Harrison and McKinley administrations set the stage for him. Then, in a defining moment, TR's superb gallantry in leading the Rough Riders' successful assault on San Juan Hill was rewarded with superb national press coverage. (Anticipating that possibility, and to his eternal political credit, TR had happened to invite several of his favorite reporters to join him as he led the Rough Riders.) The war hero was decorated the following year at age forty in 1899 with the governorship of the state of New York. Wearing his trademark Rough Riders hat to the Republican National Convention held in Philadelphia in 1900, TR received the nomination for and won the vice presidency that year. Leon Czolgosz's bullets ended President McKinley's life in 1901 and TR, descending Mt. Marcy in the Adirondacks, received the news that the presidency was to be his.

In 1854 one-term Congressman Abraham Lincoln couldn't get elected to the U.S. Senate. In 1856 he was passed over for the vice presidency on the fledgling Republican party ticket. In 1858, the year of the famous debates, he lost another bid for the U.S. Senate, this time to incumbent Democrat Stephen A. Douglas. But Abe was cultivating an issue and its time was coming. If there had been telephone polls in 1860, their results would have shown that most voters in the North and even in the border states did not believe that the institution of slavery should be permitted to expand into the western territories, especially the newly settled Kansas and Nebraska territories. The inside-the-Beltway gang, particularly Douglas, were pushing the politically convenient notion of "popular sovereignty," which meant, "Let the voters in each new territory decide for themselves whether or not they want to make slavery legal there."

In a powerful speech at the Cooper Union in New York in 1860, exhibiting new and thorough and persuasive historical evidence he had uncovered, Lincoln showed his listeners how a majority of the Founding Fathers had gone as far as they could under the circumstances to circumscribe slavery. He had dug through the records of the Continental Congress and matched antislavery votes with signers of the Declaration of Independence, concluding that a strong majority of the signers were against slavery. Today we would call this "campaign research," and there is no substitute for it when it is done well. By invoking the Founding Fathers and by not attacking the institution where it existed, however, Abe had found a moderate or mainstream approach to the defining issue of his day. From there it was just a matter of work, patience, and the good fortune that attends to the political fates of honest politicians.

Honest Abe artfully combined his moderate approach to abolitionism with his record of founding the Republican party in Illinois. He tempered the package with an image makeover from circuit lawyer to rail-splitter. And that was enough to win him the new party's presidential nomination over several formidable abolitionists from the eastern and border states.

In the four-way 1860 Douglas/John Breckenridge/John Bell/Lincoln race, Abe's end-slavery-by-the-most-moderate-means position caused him to carry the North. With the South contained and split, he finally turned the tables on Douglas and headed for the White House, and the bloodiest war in our history.

Even Strom Thurmond, the longest-serving senator in American history, couldn't get elected the first time he ran for a U.S. Senate seat. In 1950 while the governor of South Carolina, Thurmond decided to take on South Carolina Senator Olin D. Johnston. Johnston whipped him. Two years later, running as a write-in for a seat made suddenly empty in the midst of the campaign by the unexpected death of Senator Burnet Maybank, former Governor Thurmond got elected. A half-century later Thurmond was still in his Senate seat and he hadn't faced a serious challenge for a generation.

5. Coming from Behind

NO reporter ever won an award covering a blowout. A tight race, however, makes a good story. Good stories draw TV viewers and newspaper readers. That sells advertising. Reporters please their publishers, win journalism awards, and enhance their reputations covering tight races.

As a consequence of these facts of journalistic life, in the beginning stages of campaigns reporters build up challengers and tear down front-runners. They don't do it consciously, at least not for the reasons listed here. If asked in a bar after hours, many reporters would say there's a journalism ethos that requires reporters to scrutinize the front-runner most closely. After all, the front-runner's the one most likely to get the job. "And besides," the most honest ones would add, "this is America, tight races give the issues a good airing and that's good; and besides that, we Americans, the sons and daughters of immigrants, like to see the underdog given a leg up."

So start every race as the underdog. Tell the reporters why it's going to be such an uphill battle. There is a direct relationship between the margin that separates the candidates and the scrutiny of the front-runner. But too far back is too far back. You must also convince them you are viable, that you can win. To do that you must work hard and you must show you have the "fire in the belly."

There are a thousand examples. But my brother-in-law Mark

Sanford's campaigns are the best I know. He always comes from back in a crowded pack to win in the primary. Then he rides that momentum through the runoff. And when he shows up in the general, nobody knows who he is. But they say he's a phenom. And they're tired of the other guy. It's the perfect dynamic.

First he came from nowhere to win South Carolina's first congressional district in 1994. Then he came from nowhere again in 2002 to become South Carolina's 115th Governor. Here's how he does it, and the principles are exactly the same and absolutely transferable to the smallest race in the smallest district in the smallest town in Rhode Island.

First, he comes up with a couple of issues and a slogan or two that will be the basis of his message. In 1994 he ran against the federal deficit. In 2002 he said he'd restructure the state government to make it less wasteful.

Then he goes everywhere and talks to everyone who will listen to his message. But he spends nothing early in the campaign. He just walks and talks. Meanwhile, way under the radar screen, he's raising money, lots of it. Everyone else has ads running. They're opening storefronts. They have people whooping around with hats and banners. Mark drives himself everywhere and when he gets there he just walks and talks. His campaign headquarters is in the back of the family Suburban, a couple of boxes of bumper stickers and a few yard signs.

In the early debates he looks kind of surprised to be there, like maybe it was a mistake that they asked him inside where all the politicians are. He's just a regular guy. Meanwhile, his bank account is bursting.

With six weeks to go to the primary he starts dumping his money into TV. The thinking goes that the undecideds don't start paying attention until the last six weeks. Let the front-runners bruise one another up, then he'll make his move. It's a sprinter's strategy, which is appropriate for Mark because he was a schoolboy sprinter. But you don't have to be a schoolboy sprinter to make it work for you.

Think about it. He gets all the unpaid underdog stories—the man alone with his message stories—in the early and middle stages of the campaign. Then, having established that he's not slick, bought, or packaged, that he's just a hard-working guy who cares, he outbuys his opponents two or three to one during the period that the undecided voters are making up their minds.

These are the steps. They will work at the town level just as successfully as they work on a statewide level. But be careful to take them all, and in sequence. Each needs the other.

6. Friends

YOU cannot win alone. And the friends you choose to help you win will be yours for a long time, so choose them carefully.

The English language doesn't provide us with a word that describes the relationship between a politician and the other politicians and government officials with whom he or she works. "Friend" is too personal. "Acquaintance," "ally," and "associate" all imply too much distance. "Colleague" isn't bad, but it carries with it the implication that the two serve together on the same governmental entity. So we are generally left with "friend," and "friend" inevitably gets us into trouble when one of our "friends" gets into trouble. The suggestion then is that we aren't careful about picking our friends.

In fact, in large measure elected officials don't pick their friends in government in any way similar to the ways in which we choose friends and build networks in private life.

Whether it is in business, at church, at the country club, or in government, we all build networks. These networks often begin in our school years. A well-rounded and reasonably ambitious adult should have, by the time he is in his thirties, a network that includes people in virtually every sector of life. These are the friends we pick, and they are important to us. In many cases these friendships help elected officials get elected, especially the first time they run.

There are some local officials who keep a group of these supporters around them as a kind of "kitchen cabinet." A city councilman with whom I've served for over ten years now, Frank Glover, used to do this. He had a group of a half-dozen pals, including a former Beaufort police chief and a prominent realtor and the owner of the biggest real estate management firm in town and a couple of others, and, as the story goes, they'd sit around on the Tuesday mornings before Tuesday evening city council meetings and allegedly counsel Frank on how to vote on the various matters expected up that evening. There's nothing wrong with that, so long as there aren't conflicts of interest on the parts of the advisers that are undisclosed to the councilmember, and knowing those involved and, in particular, Frank, in this case I'm sure there were not.

Once installed in office, local officials find in place a whole solar system of other elected and appointed officials they should get to know and with whom they will soon find themselves working. Mayors work on regional issues with the mayors from nearby cities, and oftentimes they participate in statewide coalitions with many mayors. City council-members get to know their congressmen, the members of their county council, and the township board. School board members also become familiar, as do the members of the boards that run water districts, health boards, airports, and public transit systems. Knowing lots of people and being able to work with them is, after all, what politicians are famous for.

Party lines get in the way of these relationships. As a general rule, it's best for local officials to be nonpartisan. Sometimes it can't be helped. In Boston, be a Democrat. In Arizona, be a Republican. But in places where both Republicans and Democrats are found in significant numbers, be nonpartisan. Coming out of newspapering, and with no political aspirations beyond being mayor, I have been able to stay nonpartisan, and I've never regretted it. I have very good relationships with both of South Carolina's U.S. Senators, Lindsey Graham, a Republican, and Fritz Hollings, a Democrat. Congressman Floyd Spence, a Republican, and I had an excellent working relationship up until his death. The same was true of Strom Thurmond and me, except that he was in his nineties when our association began and I'm not sure he ever got exactly clear that I wasn't a former mayor.

When I came on Council in 1993, David Taub predicted privately to friends that I would be a disaster. He is a Democrat and time showed that we worked well together. David's neighbor, Beth Grace, one of the founders of the Republican party in Beaufort County, has been a close political ally since we worked so well together on the Highway 21 project. But David and Beth have not been allies. Party politics prevented it. I have found that when in Congress or at the state legislature, you must be from one political party or another, or else be from neither and thus be powerless. At the local level the opposite is true: the nonpartisan is able to work with everyone, and from that he derives great strength. When asked my party affiliation, I say: "I'm both." And people seem to like that.

Being both Republican and Democrat makes every election season an adventure. The longer you serve, the more you will have worked with all the office-seekers, and so the more likely it is that they will expect you to support them as inevitably they seek to move up. Soon you'll have worked with both candidates in, say, the house race for the seat in the state legislature that represents your town. It won't be long until the same is true with the congressional seat that represents your district, when a vacancy appears there. As you approach these situations, you will be reminded again that "friend" doesn't really mean friend.

In 1980 Jimmy Carter was running for reelection. The Ayatollah had taken hostage fifty-two Americans who had been trapped in the Tehran embassy, and the rescue debacle in the desert had further frightened America. The following month the Soviets invaded Afghanistan. At home, Carter had been there for New York City in the early days of Ed Koch's first term, but recently there had been broken promises as to financial aid that the president had said would be available to the city but that never actually materialized. Koch had faced several very difficult budgets, budgets in which, for example, he had had to either, at worst, lay off cops and teachers or, at best, defer their hiring. The promised, but then undelivered, federal aid would have significantly relieved the pain. Adding an additional irritant to his relationship with Koch, Carter had been wishy-washy on America's commitment to Israel, and that at a time of more-than-usual unrest in the area.

Meanwhile Ronald Reagan was showing promise as a challenger. Reagan's rhetoric on Israel was good. While there was no chance Reagan would win Democratic New York City, he had a shot at winning New York state. And if he won New York state's electoral votes, he might very well put together the electoral votes to win the presidency. As a Democrat, Koch had endorsed Carter. But Ed had also said that if the President wanted Ed to work actively for his candidacy, Carter would have to publicly shore up his stance on Israel. This was significant because Carter's pollster, Pat Caddell, had identified the Jewish vote in both New York state and in Florida as a key constituency in those two swing states. Caddell's polls showed Carter needed Koch's help in both places.

Ed had a list of four things about Israel Carter must promise to do before Ed would campaign for him. And Carter was thinking about whether he could say those four things. About that time Ronald Reagan's people called up and asked if Ed would like to meet the former California governor. Ed agreed to the meeting, and it was set for one afternoon at Gracie Mansion. The press had reported that Reagan liked jelly beans, so we got some to go on the coffee table.

The Carter people couldn't believe Ed would meet with Reagan. And neither could the New York press corps. The news was a sensation.

At the meeting Ed did just as he had promised: he filled the candidate in on the fiscal difficulties the city was encountering. Reagan, for his part, listened attentively. To the press afterwards, each said nice things about one another with Ed stopping well short of saying anything that could be interpreted as an endorsement.

What had been accomplished? First, Ed had clearly gotten Carter's attention and he would clearly be getting special handling from the Carter campaign from then on. Second, he had hedged his bet on Carter by making inroads with Reagan. Third, he had once again demonstrated to New Yorkers his independence, and New Yorkers like independence. Had he damaged himself with Democrats? Probably, and maybe that hurt him some in the 1982 Democratic gubernatorial primary, but clearly not enough to change the election's outcome. Finally, after Reagan won, Ed had entree into the Reagan White House, and in fact Reagan turned out to be a pretty good supporter of New York, something he very likely would not have been had Ed snubbed him during the campaign.

What's the message? There are several. First, picking the winner's important, and much will be forgiven you if you pick the winner. If you aren't sure who's going to win, it's okay to hedge your bet. Second, you have much more flexibility if you are non-partisan and much more still if you have no aspirations to run in the future for higher office. Third, don't give without getting. When someone is asking you for your endorsement, it is appropriate to ask for something in return. If you are looking at a close election coming up soon, you can ask for support. If you are looking to move up, you can ask for support in that effort, although it's a long shot that the commitment, even if it's given, is any good. The best thing to ask for is support for your town, especially something specific like financial support for your next park project or new police station or greenway. This requires a little forethought and sophistication. You don't want to ask for something that cannot be delivered. But you will have time. It's likely the town manager might have some thoughts about what might reasonably be promised you.

Now, how do you get the deal in writing? Handshakes aren't too good in this area because time will dull memories and inconvenient caveats may appear where once there were none. There is clearly a need here for a piece of paper. Here's how it's done. The best piece of paper is the front page of the local paper. As you make the announcement of your endorsement, you tell your side so that it appears in the same story. Of course you don't couch it as a deal. The reporters will legitimately ask you why you've made this choice. You say you're supporting so-and-so because she's a supporter of the city, in fact she's said she'll help get state money for the greenway, and then you talk about how important her support will be to the success of the greenway. Then, you turn to her in the press conference and you say: "I'm just personally gratified on behalf of Pineville that we can count on your support for our greenway." Then you pause, inviting her favorable comments about the greenway.

After the press conference, if you have a decent relationship with at least one of the reporters, as you should have, you say to that reporter: "Look, you can help Pineville out if you make sure to put her greenway comments in your story." Then, later, when she gets elected and starts waffling on the greenway money, at least you've got the story and that will help refresh her memory of what was discussed.

In addition, don't just meet with her one-on-one. Have someone else with credibility there too. Customarily from her side she'll bring a campaign aide. If you are going to ask for her support for your greenway, bring someone who can help you pitch the greenway. Then when there are foggy memories later, and previously undiscussed caveats become the subject of discussion, you'll have someone from your side offering their corroborative recollection too.

In political deals it is the second half of the deal that gets broken. So go first, if you can.

Deals get broken for many reasons, but they are most often broken because of election losses. She can't get you the greenway money if she loses the primary and goes back to being a CPA. So, once again, picking winners is important.

Not far from Beaufort is a famous Marine Corps facility, the Recruit Depot at Parris Island. In 1999 Brigadier General Steve Cheney was named to be the general in charge of Parris Island. Parris Island hosts Marine Corps boot camp for all new male recruits from east of the Mississippi River. In addition, all female

Marine recruits from throughout America are trained at Parris Island. The commanding general's job is to run the facility and to be in charge of all the Marine Corps recruiters east of the Mississippi. As is customary, the new C.G. called up the mayor of Beaufort and asked him out to the base for a cup of coffee. Steve Cheney and I got along splendidly. We were almost exactly the same age and we both loved to trade stories. Our lives had been very different: I was a young reporter covering Vietnam War protests while he was joining up. He was from the west coast. I grew up in the midwest, then moved east. He had spent a few years in the Pentagon working with then Defense Secretary Dick Cheney (no relation), and I had done some big city time in New York's city hall. While what we had done in our lives was very different, we each obviously admired what the other had done.

During Steve Cheney's two-year tour as the C.G. at Parris Island, we saw one another regularly and we always conducted the business between us with appropriate seriousness and humor. Just after Cheney relinquished his command and retired from the military, in the summer of 2001, the congressman from the Second South Carolina Congressional District, Floyd Spence, died. As unexpected vacancies always will, Spence's death set off a scramble. One surprise in the scramble was Steve Cheney's announcement that he would run in the Republican primary. Many chose to float their names early, but Cheney was the only general. He was also the only candidate from the Beaufort part of the district. The votes in the district were virtually all in the suburbs of Columbia, which is where Floyd Spence grew up and raised his family and where he came home to from Washington. Beaufort was quite clearly the stepchild of his congressional district. Knowing where the votes were, when I saw the news of Steve Cheney's announcement, I suspected he couldn't win. A couple of days after the announcement in the paper, he called me up to ask for my support. The state senator who represents the Columbia suburbs, Joe Wilson, had also announced, and Wilson would clearly be very tough to beat.

I said: "Steve, you know I like you personally, and you have a wonderful gregarious nature that will serve you well in politics. But you've chosen to get into a very tough race. I don't know Joe Wilson and he hasn't called me. Maybe he never will. And I appreciate that you have. But I have to tell you my endorsement can't just be because I like you personally. I have thirteen thousand people who live in Beaufort that I have to think about too. To serve them, I have to know you can win. You say you are taking a poll, and I think that's the best-spent money at this stage of the campaign that there can be. A good poll will tell you if there is a road map to victory and may even tell you what will be some of its twists and turns."

He said, "Yes, I'm working on a couple of the last questions now."

I said, "Good, get it just the way you want it, and then put it out there. And I'll tell you what. When you get the results back, you call me up and I'll come over because I want to be convinced that you have a chance. I'm not asking that you show me all the poll, but I'll want to see the head-to-head numbers and the recognition numbers. And in the meanwhile, if Joe Wilson calls me up, I'll tell him I'm in church and praying over my decision."

Cheney said, "Fair enough." What else could he say?

Well, he never called me. The poll must have shown him there was no way to win. It happens, and when it does the poll money is money very well spent. Instead, the day before the conclusion of the filing period, Steve announced he wouldn't be running, saying simply the race wasn't winnable.

One additional thought about this. If Steve had called me over and he'd shown me that he could win, but that he was a long shot, I would have asked to see his campaign bankbook. Because for a long shot to win, a lot of money is required, and in a short campaign the money must be raised fast and you should be able to tell after ten days or two weeks whether big sums are coming in. Even with the polling results and the facts on the money, there is plenty of uncertainty. While you are uncertain, don't plunge. Endorsements in close races are welcome right up until the final days of the campaign. Wait until your gut (and the polling numbers when you can get them) tells you which way to go, and until then hold back.

Some candidates and office-holders have too many friends, and others don't have enough. It is often a product of the times. When there has been difficulty in a local government, like when there's been publicly revealed corruption, for example, the voters are more likely to turn to an "outsider" or "new broom." This will be someone with few alliances. Conversely, when the government is perceived to be free of corruption and running competently, the voters are likely to feel comfortable with someone who knows everyone and who won't take up a lot of their time finding their way around. This will be someone with many friends.

Whether you have many, or just a few, pick them carefully. They will be with you longer than you think.

7. Money

THERE is no such thing as noncontroversial money in politics. If you use your own, you may later be criticized for "buying" the election. If you use someone else's, you may later be criticized for having been "bought" by your contributor. Yet it is also said with considerable justification that "money is the mother's milk of politics."

The first best solution to this dilemma is to spend as little money on your campaign as possible. But campaigns, especially if they involve television advertising, are expensive. And when they are close, competitors will often do whatever is necessary within the law to win. Many will also step outside the letter of the law and few will be caught. Many close elections have been decided by who spent the most money. Many others have been decided by who spent the money they had most wisely. A few will grow big and strong without mother's milk, but there's no denying at the end of the day that for most of us mother's milk helped.

There is no consolation in second place and therefore all necessary efforts must be made to achieve victory. Remember, however, the opinion-makers in your community also watch who spent what to win. You will enjoy a stronger mandate if you have won even though you were outspent. Conversely, if you outspent your opponent two to one and won narrowly, you will find it somewhat more difficult to govern.

The next best solution to the money dilemma, therefore, is to raise the money your campaign needs from as broadly based a group of contributors as possible. If you accept modest sums from many individuals in many walks of life, you will have the money you need to run your campaign responsibly while avoiding criticism.

It is equally important that, once elected, you appear to favor no individual or group with your governmental efforts and decisions. If the reporters see no indication of your toadying to any individual or group, how you raised the money for your campaign will remain a one-day story.

Contributors, whether they wrote checks or pounded in yard signs, are not entitled to favoritism.

In the 1980s there was a very good mayor of Hilton Head Island, South Carolina, named Harvey Ewing. Harvey made one mistake, however. Hilton Head Island grew more and more prosperous in the '70s and '80s, and that was fine with almost everyone. But the island itself didn't get any bigger and the town didn't grow off the island. The business community supported Mayor Ewing and he was there for them. But then in the late '80s the traffic jams started and the guys at the golf clubs started wondering to one another whether their quality of life was declining. About that time, running for reelection, Harvey was addressing a Rotary Club, and he was asked about a position the Hilton Head Chamber of Commerce had taken recently. He began his answer by saying: "People say I'm a pawn of the chamber of commerce. Well, I'm proud to be a pawn of the chamber of commerce." That line, captured on videotape, became the basis of the TV spot that Frank Chapman, a no-growth candidate from political nowhere, used to beat Harvey.

Be a toady to no one. Conversely, it is just as essential to your reelection that you not bend so far over backwards to appear fair that you discriminate against your contributors. In Washington it is said that the money buys access. At the local level everyone can have access. What then does the money buy at the local level? It buys good government. And anyone who has tried to run a business or raise a family under an incompetent or corrupt local government will tell you that competent, clean local government is worth the investment.

When entering a campaign, it is prudent to assume that the outcome will be close and that sooner or later you will find yourself in the "whatever is necessary" mode. To have available the necessary funds to stay in the race in the last sixty days, you will need to raise some serious dollars. To do that you'll need a campaign committee. You have looked at your community from the point of view of neighborhood interest groups; now look at it as an overlapping series of business interest groups. Here comes the acid test of your candidacy. Are there people from these neighborhood and business groups who will lend their names to your candidacy? Sit down with your spouse or closest supporter and diagram your community this way. If your community is racially diverse, include within your diagram the racial groups. Then put names next to each group. These names should be the names of people of stature whom you know and who you think either are or could be supporters of yours.

The next step—and here's one of the many places organizational ability, hard work, and people skills pay off—is to either call or preferably go see each of these people. Most people find it vastly easier to say no to a voice on the phone than to a person sitting in their living room. So whenever possible, go see your prospective committee members in their homes. When you get there, don't be shy. Pitch the wife. Pitch the kids. Pitch the mother-in-law. Tell the son that you're running and how important his father's support is to your candidacy. Watch the movie *Primary Colors* and learn from the Bill Clinton character. The ability to make an ordinary person feel extraordinary is a high political art. If you weren't born with this talent, seek to acquire it. An ordinary ego can be intoxicated by flattery, and an intoxicated ego will pledge things that defy rationality. In this way you can build something from nothing.

A campaign committee, or organized and energized campaign supporters who are individuals of stature in your community, is invaluable in many ways. They can keep the "buzz" good in the coffee and barber shops, and they can tell you when the buzz isn't good for you. They can bring back early news of possible defections to or nastiness by your opponent. They can suggest initiatives you may wish to propose as a part of your campaign. They can tell you early when you've made a mistake, early enough for you still to correct it.

Many of your committee members, when they are properly motivated, will also help you raise money. Here's where the business community comes in. Every town has a major employer. It may be a factory, or a military installation, or an industry. Let's take Indianapolis, Indiana, for an example. Eli Lilly and Company, the pharmaceutical giant, is headquartered there. Whole blocks of downtown are taken up by pill factories. Tens of thousands of Indianapolis residents work for Lilly. In the past generation, many insurance companies have moved their headquarters to Indianapolis too. The insurance companies also employ thousands. There is also the speedway and the sports teams. The place is car crazy—there must be fifty car dealerships there as well. To raise money for a run for the Indianapolis City Council, you would put together a finance subcommittee of your campaign committee with representatives from each of these business sectors. It would then be up to the Lilly person to organize a fundraiser or fundraisers at his or her house for the Lilly executives. Similarly, your car dealer representative would put something together for the car dealers. It would be up to that person to know whether to mix the GM people with the Ford people, just as the sports person would make the call as to whether to try to host something for each sport individually or whether to try to get all the sports honchos into one room.

The day of the sports reception, sit down with your sports person and go through the list of who's coming. These people have egos that may be bigger even than yours. Learn about them so that when you shake their hand that evening you can convey immediately to them that you not only know who they are, but that you are an admirer of theirs. Each will thus become an admirer of yours. This is one of those many places in public life where it helps to like people. If you genuinely like people and don't think you're better than all of them, then getting to know these sports people will be a genuine pleasure for you. If it is, it'll show. If you're just faking it, that may show as well.

At these gatherings it is customary for the candidate to give a five-to-ten-minute pitch. The standard format (after publicly thanking and complimenting the host) is to begin with a humorous campaign story. Then move into some "inside" campaign news that illustrates how close the race is (and therefore implicitly how important it is that money be raised). That part is followed by a short piece on what the campaign's all about and why you will represent the people in the room better than your opponent will. My custom is never to mention my opponent's name. That doesn't mean you can't deride his message using phrases like "others say" and "when you hear people in this town say." That brings you to the explicit appeal, which is customarily a rendition of the cost of TV time and some self-serving data about what you and your opponent have raised and what your goals are. The close ought to be along the lines of expressing the importance of the sports community to the economic well-being of the city. This is intended to make those present feel they have a civic responsibility to get involved in the race. In the mingling before and after the pitch, it is all right to talk about the importance of money to the campaign, but it would be unusual to put the arm on the prospective donors yourself. Leave that to your sports person, but make sure he does it.

If the race is tight and election day is coming soon, you may have to do some direct soliciting, however. You will probably use the privacy of the telephone for this. In 1977, when Ed Koch first ran for mayor, he started the race sixth in a field of seven, a very difficult position from which to try to raise the kind of dollars a candidate needs to get on and stay on TV. Virtually every dollar the campaign raised went to television. At the end of the primary campaign, Ed eked his way into a runoff with Mario Cuomo. The Koch campaign was flat broke, and with the runoff election ten days away, there was no time to organize receptions. The only option was to sit Ed down for an hour each afternoon between campaign stops and have him call donors directly. The need was in the neighborhood of $50,000 to $100,000 a day. Once he'd raised it, he could go back out handshaking. A couple of days of that and you find out deep in your soul how badly you want the office. Ed is as tough as they come and he prevailed in the all-important Democratic party runoff ten days later.

Your supporters and staffers can solicit contributions for you, but no matter how hard they may work for you, they are not you and they cannot raise for you what you can raise for yourself. In a tight race, you should keep the big givers for yourself.

Nine elections out of ten it is impossible to get elected mayor of Indianapolis without the support of the executives at Eli Lilly and Company. The same is true in virtually every other "company town." Of nine elections, four may be close, and it is likely the executives will support both sides in the close elections.

Only under very unusual circumstances should a mayor be even lukewarm about the major employer in his or her town. These businesses are what make things tick. Campaign contributions is just a part of how the company brass wield their power. All the election reform laws in the world notwithstanding, the word goes out into the workforce which candidate will be best for the company. And most of the company's employees vote for the candidate who enjoys that buzz around the water coolers.

Under normal circumstances, elected officials should be boosters or cheerleaders for their town's core businesses. If the major employer is a hundred small businesses, then the officials should be boosters for entrepreneurism. If it's a military or other government installation, they should be a booster for that. But boosters are not toadies. When it comes to regulating the largest employer in town, work with them but do not work for them.

Your success as a booster will have fundraising implications. In Indianapolis, for example, if you have been there for Lilly, the insurance companies, the sports teams, and the car dealers, you'll raise more money. If you've been silent, you'll raise less. If you've been critical of one or another of those sectors, you'll raise less still. This is not to say you shouldn't be critical when it's warranted, it is just to say you should understand the financial implications of what you're doing.

If you've been correctly critical when it was warranted even if it stung, and you have shown you will be a booster when it is warranted, the executives will respect you and treat you with caution. But they will not write checks to you that are as big as the checks they will write to the toadies. My own view is that that is all right. In the TV age, public officials live by their wits. Your independence will draw you money from individual donors, and more important, it will earn you the respect of the voters, who as a group have little respect for toadies. Even the water cooler crowd at the company respects independence.

A campaign committee is a very flexible entity, and there have been a wide variety of positions created at campaign committees to fit various circumstances. But there is one position that is essential: the treasurer. No matter how small your committee is, fill this slot. The campaign treasurer's position should be filled by a prominent lawyer or banker in town who has some street sense, who is willing to do a little real work on a pro bono basis on your behalf, and who enjoys your full confidence. You should know the state laws that govern campaign finances, and your treasurer should know them too. Your treasurer should be in charge of getting the filings correct and in on time, and you should make sure he or she does. But there's more.

Here's why the treasurer's the most important person in your campaign. There will inevitably be questions from reporters about money. These will be some of the most uncomfortable questions the campaign will face. If you don't have a campaign treasurer, you will be facing them unprotected. But if you have a campaign treasurer who has some savvy, he or she can insulate you somewhat from the heat. If a mistake's been made, the treasurer made it. The treasurer is the first line of defense.

The kinds of campaign contributions that cause particular trouble fall generally into two categories. Contributions from individuals with criminal records or from people who are known to be shady can cause trouble. So can medium and large contributions from individuals or businesses doing profitable business with the city, especially if you have somehow already been linked to these donors. The reporters will want to pin the trouble on you, but it will be harder for them to make it stick if you have a treasurer who's willing to be out there taking responsibility. The treasurer's standard line is that it was an oversight. "The check came in in the mail and we put it in the bank, thanks for pointing it out, we've sent the money back," or words to that effect. The rules are simple in this confidential partnership. If it's good, you did it. If it's bad, the treasurer did it. A good treasurer is someone who can follow those rules.

The most prized post-victory appointments are often reserved for the campaign treasurers of successful campaigns. You may even notice that they are often the first announced appointments. That's because the newly elected official gave his treasurer carte blanche.

If they can save you trouble, they can cause you trouble too. When Koch ran in 1977, not only did he have difficulty raising big money, but the powerbrokers he asked to serve as his campaign treasurer took a look at what they perceived to be his chances and declined the opportunity. Being pragmatic, Ed took the best he could get, a businessman named Bernard Rome.

Following by default my rule number one, Ed didn't raise much money so he didn't have to answer many questions. In addition, following by default my rule number two, the money from the entrenched New York interests, real estate management and Wall Street, didn't give his candidacy much of a chance so they didn't give his candidacy much money. Accordingly, the chances that Rome would have to cover for Ed were further decreased.

During Ed's transition period, Rome put in for the chairmanship of the Off-Track Betting Board, and Ed appointed him to the job. The Off-Track Betting Board, or OTB as it is known, is very political because of the tightness with which this government-sponsored gambling concern is regulated by New York State. Bernie Rome the businessman thrived for a little while at OTB, until he had an idea about how OTB could make more money and how the state legislature was holding it back. He wanted Ed's help in getting the state's gambling laws changed. The city's lobbyist in Albany took a look at Rome's proposal and told Ed it was dead on arrival in Albany. Being pragmatic, Ed relayed the lobbyist's message right to Rome, who became infuriated.

From that moment on Ed found himself in a public fight with his former campaign treasurer. That was the bad news. The good news was there hadn't been any funny business in the campaign so there weren't any skeletons in the campaign's closet that Rome could drag out. In the end Ed had to remove him from the chairmanship. Ed's line was great. "What more do you need to know about me to show you that I am an honest guy," he asked the city hall press corps at the press conference where they came at him with Rome's most vicious words, "than that I can fire my own campaign treasurer?"

Jack Kennedy said, "The White House isn't a good place to make new friends." City hall isn't that bad, but it holds its own dangers. When you gain power, you will also gain a retinue of new acquaintances. As during your campaign you familiarized yourself with the state campaign finance laws, soon after you are elected you should familiarize yourself with the state ethics laws. We all must feed our families. The public understands that, and they will readily forgive you the time you take away from your public responsibilities so that you can earn the money to support your family. But your constituents will never forgive you for directly using your public position to make money.

The only legitimate reason to enter public life is to render a service to the public, and many elected officials truly have come to serve, and it will be quickly obvious to you as you work with them day-to-day that they are the best. Others enter public life, however, because they wish to be loved. They are easily recognizable because they talk too much, but they are not dangerous.

The danger all comes from the third group: those who gained office so that they can create opportunities for themselves to make money. You will not mistake the members of this group for a member of the second group, because they will say little. For a time you may mistake one of them for a member of the first group because they understand the value of the public service rhetoric. If you listen closely to the buzz in the coffee shops, however, you will generally hear of them coming close to the ethics violation line before they go over the line. As they come close, they put out signals of their willingness to engage in shady activities, and those signals bring to them more such opportunities, until it is only a matter of time before they actually go over the line. Although only the clumsy ones will ever be chastened by the state ethics commission, much less the courts, most will receive as their punishment the loss of esteem for them by a community that once placed its trust in them.

Local government is the government that is closest to the people. Local government officials, then, have the opportunity to make changes that are felt immediately by the people. The area under a widow's house is being flooded in a rainstorm and she calls you for help. The water is rising and, she says, it will soon be seeping through her floors. You call the town manager and demand that he dispatch a public works crew to clean out the catch basin in front of her house. Reluctantly three city workers throw a crowbar and some shovels and rakes in the back of a city pickup, pull on their slickers, and drive over to the widow's house. After a few minutes they remove the blockage. The flood under her house subsides as the rain swirls down the storm drain. The town manager calls you back to say the crew solved the problem. You hear nothing from the widow until she needs something else six months later.

Did helping her out in the rainstorm put money in your pocket? No. Did it give you more satisfaction than selling another car on a Saturday afternoon, or writing another insurance policy? If it did, you'll make it in local government.

8. Campaign Bumps

CAMPAIGNS function as public testing grounds for prospective elected officials. Campaigns present a host of challenges to candidates. The qualities they test are many of the qualities elected officials find tested during the time they hold public office.

Campaigns test the integrity of candidates, and elected officials must resist constant pressure to say one thing to one group and another to another. Campaigns test resilience, and public life requires resilience. Campaigns test discretion, and public service requires discretion. Campaigns test the ability of candidates to master information quickly. The elected official's landscape is heaped with data that must be assimilated and applied, sometimes quickly, to decision-making. Campaigns test management skills, and office-holders should be good managers. Campaigns often reveal the genuine humility or arrogance of candidates. In the rough-and-tumble world of public life, self-confidence and a positive self-image are essential, and a vigorous campaign will reveal those qualities as well. Campaigns test candidates' good general health and hearty constitutions. And those too, when meetings run late or travel arrangements get messy, are beneficial attributes. Finally, a campaign tests a candidate's sense of humor, and there is no single personal quality more helpful in public life than a sense of humor.

In the give and take of debates and forums, humor can be used like a sword. It is the most effective of all weapons. Back at campaign headquarters, where a team of strangers has been assembled in a common cause, at those moments when prospects seem bleak and volunteers are considering their exit strategies, nothing will staunch the bleeding like a kind word and a laugh.

Doctors get a laugh or two around the hospital. Lawyers get a few around the courthouse. Most offices have a comedian or two who can keep things light. But there is nowhere like a campaign headquarters to present the varieties of situations and the human comedy in raw form. Here one finds vanity, generosity, greed, ambition, artifice, coincidence, conspiracy, brilliance, and stupidity all on parade and on deadline. The best paid and most experienced campaign planners in the country find themselves dealing with the unexpected most of the time. Politicians like life on the edge. Some would say many of us need to be confronted with calamity to do our best work. Campaigns test this quality— grace under pressure—as well.

Henry Hudson and I had worked together on several community projects in the two years before I first ran for mayor of Beaufort. A wonderful and engaging barber, Mr. Hudson as I always call him, had spent some time doing civil rights work somewhere. When I said I would run, he said he would help me. While I had endorsements from some black leaders, there were only a few local members of the African-American community who actually volunteered their time. Mr. Hudson had said for weeks that he knew the importance of phone calls and was going to come in and start making them. I always encouraged him, but I didn't want to push him too hard. Well, about a week before election day he showed up and said it was time to start making calls. Did I have a list of phone numbers? Most of the black voters, as well as some of the town's richest white folks who own the big houses along the Beaufort River, live in Beaufort precinct 1-B. So I asked Katherine Grace to print Mr. Hudson out a list of the 1-B voters.

As you read across the horizontal line of the printout, the database provides the precinct, the last name, the first name, the street address, the voter registration number, the gender, and the race of the voter. With the exception of the voter registration number, which is assigned by the board of elections, all this information is the information the voter supplies the government when he or she registers to vote. It's all public information, and pollsters buy it from the board of elections when they prepare to take a poll. Then there's a field in which to place any comments like "undecided" or "hates traffic," information gleaned from previous phone calls. On the race line white voters are designated with a W, Hispanic voters get an H, Oriental voters get an O, and African-American voters are designated by a B. Being always sensitive about race, neither Katherine nor I explained to Mr. Hudson what the codes meant, and he just started calling right from the top of the first page. We didn't think anything of it.

I was across the hall in my office making calls, as were several other people, making calls from fax machines and on any other phone lines that worked. After an hour or so I went in to see how my friend was doing.

"How's it going?" I asked.

"Good, good," he said. "I'm finding some folks home."

"Have any of them ever heard of me?"

"Some," he said.

"Any going to vote for me?"

"Yeah, well I'm telling them. And they're listening."

"Any not going to vote for me?"

"Yeah, there was this one that isn't," he said, running his finger down the call list. It was Joe Mix. Joe's one of the white folks who lives on the river. He is also probably Henry Chambers's best friend. Henry was my major opponent in the race. Henry and Joe share offices. They invest together. From all the talk on the street, Joe was up to his eyeballs in Henry's campaign. And they were cocky.

About six thoughts went through my mind at once. The first was it's amazing what strangers will tell strangers over the telephone. Another was that Mr. Hudson was really working and was really telling me the flat-out truth, two things that were proven again and again over the following week. Another was that I wished I could have been a third party on that call because both Joe Mix and Henry Hudson were smart, strong-willed advocates for their respective candidates, and I would have enjoyed hearing the lines they threw at one another in their short time together.

I also thought of a story Ed Koch told me. There's usually a time in a tight race when the two campaigns unexpectedly bump up against each other. Early in Ed's public life, he was a one-term city councilman running for Congress in the famous silk stocking district that includes the toniest neighborhoods on Manhattan's east side. Congressman John Lindsay, an Upper East Side resident, quit the seat after he got elected mayor of New York, and City Councilman Ed Koch, a Greenwich Village resident, resolved to move up and fill the vacancy.

A street campaigner by nature and necessity, Ed hit the subway stops, standing at the top of the stairs and shaking hands and exchanging one-liners with commuters as they rushed by. He was running against a guy named Whitney North Seymour, Jr., who was the son of a well-known civil rights lawyer and who was himself at that time the state senator representing the Upper East Side in Albany. Seymour had made it known to his friends that he wanted ultimately to be governor. There were fifteen or so subway stops in the district and Ed had been working them since May.

Some time right after Labor Day, Ed was standing at one of the Fourteenth Street stops when Seymour pulled up in his big campaign station wagon. He got out of the car and walked up to Ed and asked him: "How long have you been doing this? And what time did you get here?" The questions were undoubtedly intended simply to make small talk along the lines of "How was the movie?"

Displaying two of the characteristics that would later make him a political legend, his in-your-face cockiness and an instinct for twisting the question around to the one he wished most to answer, Ed replied: "All year, and I start at seven a.m."

As he told it to me: "At that moment a look came over Seymour's face that showed that he now knew he could lose the race."

I also wondered whether, as he had set down the telephone, that look had come over Joe Mix's face.

9. Going Negative

IN the six weeks before election day, candidates in local races should spend the hour or so they are allocated in public forums talking about how they will improve the lives of their constituents. They may also spend a few minutes speaking of what good they've already done, and briefly outlining any other personal qualifications that might get them some votes. Under no circumstances should a candidate in a local race disparage one of his or her opponents at a forum or in a debate. Likewise, bad-mouthing opponents to reporters should be avoided. No matter how delicately it can be done, bad-mouthing comes off as nasty.

This is not to say, however, that the little known unfortunate things there are about your opponent should be concealed from the electorate. Just the opposite. The more of her dirty laundry that can be hung out, the better it is for you. It is just that none of it should be hung by you.

Get someone else who is unconnected to you to do the dirty work. The enemy of your enemy is your friend. And in this particular endeavor, if there is anyone who is your girl, it is most likely to be she.

If you haven't hired a pollster to do some of this for you, then by now you should have picked up from the local elections board a copy of their list of registered voters for your district. You should also have gone through it with a couple of your most trusted friends to determine who is for you, who is against you, and who you're not sure about. With a month to go, you should have accomplished this exercise. Even in the smallest races there are sure to be voters you don't know. Consider them undecideds. In a larger race you should have raised the money to conduct a poll to test your message, and you should have the results back with two months to go. That poll will tell you who are many, but not all, of the likely voters who have not yet made up their minds. Don't bother telling the people who you know will be voting for your opponent anything bad about your opponent. You won't swing their vote. Likewise, don't incur the expense of telling those who will be voting for you what's not good about your opponent.

Negative messages should be directed solely at the undecideds. They should be delivered in the form of a sincere-sounding "Dear Voter" letter from someone who has no connection to you. And they should be delivered by the U.S. Mail in the last week of the campaign. Depending upon how well they are conceived, a negative message mailing can swing 5 to 8 percent of the total vote.

This is an area of great controversy and delicacy. So let me be as clear as I can be about the rules of engagement, which of course by their very nature change a little with every campaign season. Everything you do here will be scrutinized, and if you win and you have broken these rules, it will hurt you as you seek to govern. Negative messages must not be defamatory or gossipy. They must also be rigorously true. Sexual practices are off-limits and counterproductive. The messages that you, however anonymously, bring to the public must be legitimate and they must distinguish you from your opponent. If your opponent was cited by the board of ethics, but you were too, it's the pot calling the kettle black and it's off-limits. But if she was cited, and it can be shown, and you weren't cited, then that is a legitimate area for public discussion and a "no fingerprints" mailing.

In 1999, as the Beaufort mayoral campaign made the turn on to the final stretch, there were three of us still standing. The former mayor, Henry Chambers, according to the word on the street, was out front, and Councilwoman Donnie Beer and I were neck-and-neck in the dust at the back. Henry, who had stepped down after nineteen years as mayor in 1991, had worked in the 1980s and '90s as a real estate agent. After he left office, he brokered the sale of a barrier island known locally as Bay Point. Seventy-five or so acres in size, mostly pines and windswept sand dunes, Bay Point lies directly across the mouth of the Port Royal Sound from Hilton Head Island. There is no bridge there and the soil is sandy, which makes it hard to build anything there. But Henry is a gifted salesman and he has made a career of selling and reselling Bay Point, each time for a few million dollars more.

In 1998 Beaufort County passed a series of growth management laws that further complicated the process Henry's new owners would have to utilize to get their development plans approved. But Henry is a can-do guy and he was undeterred by the new hoops as he set out to complete them late that year. His strategy was to make use of whatever permits had already been gained in past efforts as "grandfathered" and then to "jam through" the approval process whatever other permits were needed.

As a part of the jamming through process, Henry tried to muscle everyone who stood in his way. Some samplings of

Henry's hot rhetoric appeared in the newspapers as reporters covered his appearances before various boards and commissions. One newspaper reader was a young man on St. Helena Island who believed with great sincerity and conviction that Bay Point was too fragile a barrier island to be developed. He looked up and down the coast in the vicinity of Beaufort and he saw barrier islands creeping one way and another as barrier islands will. Some featured houses hanging into the ocean where the beach had eroded under them. Others were characterized by great wide beaches that had replenished themselves. The young man was personally affronted by Henry's plans, and particularly by Henry's use of rough tactics to get his way.

As the mayoral campaign heated up, the young man contacted me through an intermediary I trusted. The young man's agenda was clear: to stop Henry from again becoming mayor. As the intermediary and I talked, it occurred to me that I should provide the young man with a list of the undecideds (including their addresses) I knew about. If he wanted to send them a letter outlining Henry's transgressions, as he perceived them, that was his business.

The letter, I was told, arrived the Thursday before the Tuesday election day. It was sincere in tone, but very rough on Henry. How do you respond? If you're the maligned candidate, you don't know how many of these letters are out there. If it's just a few, you don't want to elevate it. If it's hundreds or thousands, you have to throw together an ad, and the newspapers' deadlines have probably passed. Maybe you can still get on the radio. In the end, in this case, Henry chose not to elevate it.

At the least, the letter threw the Chambers campaign off balance the final weekend. More likely the letter cost Henry some votes. Did those votes go to Mrs. Beer or to me? We'll never know. Would I do it again?

You bet.

When you're running against experienced candidates, you give up advantages at your peril. If the race is worth getting into, it's worth winning.

PART TWO

Holding Power

10. Symbols

NOW you've won. When you, the winner, take office, the press will be interested in your "opening gesture" or "first official act." It is generally the view of reporters and editors that there is a revealing relevance in the first thing a new executive does.

Sometimes there is. My own experience has been that usually there isn't. The smart elected official will, however, capitalize on this public relations opportunity and use it to make a statement that strengthens her ability to govern. Governing is, after all, essentially getting the herd running the way you want them to so that you will have support as you seek to make better those things you came to improve. Public relations—or press management—is how elected officials keep their constituents knowing what their leaders want known. While it is likely that there will be many times in the upcoming months that you will be in the papers and on TV, it is also true that few to none of those opportunities will provide you an equal opportunity to "define yourself."

On the day of his inauguration to his first term, Ed Koch rode the bus down Broadway from his apartment in Greenwich Village to city hall. This gesture sent two signals: that he was just a regular guy leaving his apartment and going to work, and that, even though there was a car and driver at his disposal, he was choosing to place his faith in the city's embattled public transit system.

Why the bus?

Ed could have taken the N train from Eighth Street to City Hall Park. But in 1978, as the city continued to reel from its brush with bankruptcy, the subway stations featured homeless men aggressively panhandling. There was grafitti all over everything, and the stench of urine in some corridors was nearly overwhelming. Had they been able to successfully negotiate those impediments to decency, however, the new mayor's party (including about thirty reporters and cameramen) might also have had to endure an embarrassing wait of up to forty minutes for an oft-delayed local train.

At such a moment, inevitably the pack would begin feeding off of the system's decaying carcass by asking the new mayor what he intended to do to bring relief to the straphangers. Too much of that in the next day's papers would result in a mixed message. Simply put, if Ed was there to show he was a regular subway rider, then he shouldn't be talking about how he intended to overhaul the whole subway system. That's called "stepping on your own headline."

So Ed stayed above ground on his Inauguration Day, and took the bus, and he stood all the way downtown while the reporters took the seats, and the perception of him as a regular guy who wanted to live in his apartment rather than fancy Gracie Mansion stuck to his public persona for the next twelve years.

Bill Clinton's introductory shot was classic political misjudgment. In the days immediately following his inauguration, President Clinton proposed an executive order that would ban discrimination against gay people in the nation's military. On that one, not only was the message wrong, but the way it fit with its messenger was the worst. In the campaign Clinton had been roundly criticized as a draft-dodger, especially when he was compared to his opponent, George Bush, a fighter pilot in World

War II. Instead of helping his administration get going, the announcement raised all the same questions Clinton had just buried by winning the election.

More successful was Mark Sanford's first week in the Congress. Sanford had run for the First District of South Carolina seat, which includes Charleston, and pulled off some surprising upsets on his way to being included in Newt Gingrich's freshman "Contract With America" Republican class of 1994.

A fiscal conservative, Sanford had sworn, as he rang a thousand doorbells, that he would use the power of his office first and foremost to call for the elimination of the federal deficit. His bumper stickers featured his name and the word DEFICIT with a slash through it.

True to his frugal ways, Sanford spent his first night as a congressman sleeping on his office floor. During his tenure in Washington (which was only six years because of a self-imposed term limit), Sanford voted consistently against government spending, even improvements in his own district, and the federal budget was actually balanced and some of the national debt was paid off. It is unclear how much of that is due to Sanford and the Congress's efforts, and how much was a coincidental benefit of the roaring national economy of the 1990s.

No matter, ten years later the way South Carolinians regard Mark Sanford is as that guy who works so hard and is so tight with the taxpayers' money that he sleeps on his office floor.

11. Getting Started

AS I approached my own inauguration I couldn't settle on a gesture that was appropriate and yet not corny. So I decided simply to try to get put into office without a press mishap, and then get right to work. Because the city council had decided to rearrange its election schedule so as to get on the federal schedule, I only had seventeen months before I would have to run again. Even congressmen get twenty-four months, and they feel like they're in a non-stop campaign.

Mayors can often, but by no means always, control the issues the government is pursuing aggressively, or "has on the front burner," as the saying goes.

In my campaign for mayor, I said Beaufort is faced with an emerging traffic congestion problem. For the first time, motorists are sitting stopped in traffic along Boundary Street. This was only partially true. It would have been more true to say that occasionally these days when the drawbridge is open, or there are fender benders on Boundary Street, there may be traffic backups. But that was less dramatic, and I was seeking to make a point, so the hyperbole was useful.

Having been so involved in the Highway 21 on St. Helena Island controversy, though, I worried that my opponents would blame me for the emerging traffic congestion in Beaufort. So I hit upon an issue that not only resonated throughout the community, but that also blunted the charge that I was soft on traffic solutions.

Readers will recall the majestic swing-span bridge over the Intracoastal Waterway that connects the historic downtown section of Beaufort with Lady's Island, the opening section of the seventeen-mile drive to the beach. That bridge, known locally as the Woods Memorial Bridge, is owned by the South Carolina Department of Transportation, formerly known as the highway commission. However, by federal statute its schedule of openings is dictated by the U.S. Coast Guard.

For many years there had been no openings schedule at all. Sailboats came along the waterway. They sounded their horns, and the attendant swung the bridge. As Lady's Island became more and more developed and traffic counts increased, a group of local leaders lobbied the Coast Guard for a schedule, and in the early '90s, after three years of their efforts, the so-called "20 minute schedule" was imposed. But the bridge tenders followed this "three times per hour" schedule casually, and the result was that motorists still didn't know when the bridge would be open. Complicating things further, in late 1998 the bridge was being repaired, so that meant more delays and uncertainty.

All this, I perceived, created a climate for change. About a year before the election, long before I announced my candidacy, I staked out my territory: People need to know when the bridge is going to be open so they can make their plans when to come and go, I said. The traffic at the bridge is out of hand.

If you want genuine support, you always have to have something for people to do. If they actually do something, no matter how modest, then they're with you for the duration. So I made up a form letter that could be sent to Senators Fritz Hollings and Strom Thurmond and to Congressman Floyd Spence, a Democrat and two Republicans, calling on them to help the city impose upon the Coast Guard an "only twice per hour" bridge opening schedule. Helpfully, Hollings and Spence were running for reelection. I called them all up and told them what we were doing. My friend Beth Grace made up a petition and left it at places like the visitor's center and in various stores around town. It called for an "on the hour and half-hour" permitted openings schedule with two hours of no openings at the morning and evening rush hours. I kept a stack of the letters in my car with me, and whenever I got stuck at the bridge, I'd get out of the car and talk to the other motorists and pass out the letters.

Knowing there was a daily five o'clock opening that really blocked up traffic, I'd also go down to the bridge some days at five o'clock sharp and walk from car to car. It was street campaigning at its best and people loved it, even my most determined opponent, Paul Trask, who owns the movie theaters. Now here's a guy who really doesn't like traffic jams. When I came upon him one day backed up for the bridge, he said, "If you can get something done about this, even I'll vote for you."

Getting something done was, in fact, easier than anyone, including me, ever expected. The trick was to influence the Coast Guard. As it happened, Senator Hollings was on the Senate Commerce Subcommittee that had oversight of the Coast Guard's budget. During Hollings's 1998 reelection campaign, he came through Beaufort to march in the Water Festival Parade, and I arranged a meeting with him and some local businessmen who wanted to see something done about the bridge schedule. At the meeting, the senator said he'd get it changed. He didn't say how or when, and we didn't ask. That November, Hollings beat Congressman Bob Inglis by a wide margin (including in Beaufort), and in January he got to work on the bridge schedule. January is when the various federal agencies come to their respective congressional subcommittees for "authorization." The process includes a comment period, during which the agencies' congressional liasons and the Senate staffers go over any trouble spots. That's when the key senators wield their power.

You could hear the anguished screams all the way down in Beaufort. Before January 1999, a formerly smug Charleston-based bureaucrat in the Coast Guard's Bridge Section, Bruce Pruitt, wouldn't even return my phone calls. Now here he was on the other end of the phone asking to know what was the problem. Joe Maupin from Senator Hollings's office had worked it beautifully. He had been detailed by the senator to get this done for Beaufort, and, having changed the hours on a couple of bridges up in the Charleston area, he knew how the system worked. The first step toward change was to get the Coast Guard to request the bridge opening logs and traffic counts from my old friends at the South Carolina Department of Transportation.

When DOT furnished the Coast Guard with the raw vehicular and boat traffic data, I asked for a copy. I suspected the Coast Guard's statisticians—if that's what you would call them—would manipulate the figures to show what the Coast Guard wanted shown, namely that there were actually not enough openings for all the boat traffic and that the vehicular traffic tie-ups really weren't so bad. That wasn't going to work for me. The motorists were the ones I represented on the city council, and they were the ones who would be voting in the upcoming mayoral election. The sailors come from all over the world, but the motorists live in Beaufort. Besides, the motorists are trying to get their kids to school and then get to work on time, and the sailors are out for a good time. So I decided the motorists needed their own statisticians. I called up my friend Sheila Tombe, who teaches literature at the college. She led me to two teachers of statistics: Billy Cordray and Ron Harshbarger. Truly public-spirited and fed up with the bridge-related traffic jams that many days stretched through the college's campus, they agreed to analyze the data on a pro bono basis. After several meetings during which we discussed what the numbers showed and what might be palatable, we devised what I termed "the workingman's schedule": no openings on weekdays between 7:30 and 9:00 in the morning; openings on the hour and half-hour during the working day, if necessary; and no openings between 4:30 and 6:30 on weekday evenings.

According to Joe Maupin, it was a proposed schedule that was as generous to the motorist as any in South Carolina. I didn't really expect us to get the schedule approved by the Coast Guard, but in negotiating it's always a good idea to begin at the most extreme position that could be described as reasonable and then kick and scream while being pulled into a compromise. But to my surprise there was no effort at compromise on the part of the Coast Guard. They proposed, instead, to "test" the Cordray-Harshbarger schedule for ninety days—as it happened, three months before the May 1999 mayoral election. At the same time, the construction on the bridge was completed.

The effect of the new schedule and the completion of the construction was to give the Beaufort motorist the sense that all of a sudden traffic at the bridge was much better. And since I had been so out in front of the issue, I was credited with the improvement. I now had a traffic congestion victory to talk about during the campaign that was all mine and that countered whatever residue lingered from the U.S. 21 controversy that I was antimotorist. The bridge won me a lot of votes, and when they were all counted, I won the mayorality rather easily. Four years later people still thank me for what I did there.

I tell the bridge story to illustrate three points. First, if you work hard, sometimes you'll get lucky. On timing, this was as just plain lucky as it could have been. Second, it's vital for the local officials to understand how their government fits in with all the other governments, and each county across America is unique. The effective elected official cultivates ties to all governments because, in the course of a year, the official will have need of working with all other governments and many outside agencies on one issue or another. Third, and related, it's helpful for the local official to have ties to both political parties.

I was having dinner with Chicago Mayor Richard M. Daley a couple of months later, and we spoke of the same thing. Aside from the Kennedys, the Daleys are about as Democratic a family as America knows. Yet, as a prosecutor Daley developed very strong ties to Republican leaders, particularly in the Chicago suburbs. That made it possible for him, he told me, to form a close relationship with President George Bush after Daley got elected mayor. And yet Daley was deft enough to get back on his old Democratic party horse during the '91 Bush-Clinton race so as to position himself and his city as Clinton-style "New Democrats." Both the relationship with Bush and the affinity with Clinton brought millions of extra dollars into Chicago.

Local officials in cities big and small deal infrequently with the litmus test national party issues like abortion and defense. Their problems are more practical and less ideological. As fusion New York Mayor Fiorello LaGuardia put it, "There's no Republican or Democratic way to pick up the garbage."

In my case, getting down to work meant setting the new bridge times in stone and then moving on. It also meant showcasing what I do best: working with whomever wherever it is necessary to get results.

12. Clear the Table

IN June 1999, the City of Beaufort faced several lawsuits that had been lingering for several years. My predecessor, David Taub, set the table for me in this respect. David is a good friend and I like him a great deal. We served together for six years, he as mayor and I as one of the four other councilmembers, before he stepped down. But even David would acknowledge that, although he has many strengths, sitting down with his adversaries, listening to them, and crafting a compromise with them is probably not one of them.

The first lawsuit had to do with noise. Back in the 1980s, after being pressured by shopkeepers, the council under David's leadership had become fed up with noise downtown. In addition to the amplified car music that residents of American cities have had to endure in various forms in recent years, the people downtown found themselves in the '80s and '90s being preached at by missionaries. Each year there were more missionaries and it seemed each year that their voices became louder. At times their message was said to be antiwomen, anti-Semitic, or anti-Christmas. The city knew it could not control these preachers' messages, but it hoped it could somehow limit the noise level of the shouting.

Why all the fervor? A clergyman, the Reverend Karl Baker, leader of the Calvary Baptist Church in Shell Point, just outside the city's limits, was running a school for missionaries and requiring his students to preach the gospel on street corners to the general public. Sometimes they went to Savannah, but most often they came to Beaufort. Baker himself led the way. An ex-Marine who favors dark suits and cowboy boots, and who is built like a fireplug, Baker can growl out the gospel so that it can be heard for several city blocks.

In 1990 the city council passed a noise ordinance modeled on the noise ordinance of the City of Eanes, Maryland. The new law used as its criterion whether a merchant's right to conduct business in an orderly fashion was being compromised by noise emanating from the streets outside. If a merchant complained to the police, the police would come down and listen. If the noise was disruptive, the officer went outside to warn the source of the noise that he or she was about to get cited under the noise ordinance. If the noise continued unabated, or was resumed at a similar level, the offender was arrested and jailed.

No sooner had the city enacted the new law than street preachers flocked into Beaufort from hundreds of miles around to get themselves arrested in protest of the new law. They maintained their constitutional rights of free speech and freedom of religion were being unlawfully limited. The city sought relief and protection based on the Eanes case. Both sides received pro bono offers from public interest law firms that specialized in either First Amendment or neighborhood rights cases. Each side also paid large sums to their lead counsel. The street preachers' lawyer was a guy named Orin Briggs, a street preacher himself. The city's was the City Attorney Bill Harvey, son of Brantley.

Thus the matter crept through the state and federal courts during the early and mid-'90s. During the six years I was on Council before I was elected mayor, we would receive periodic reports from the legal front: "We're winning. We lost that round, but we're still winning. We won that round, but there are storm clouds. The judge doesn't know what to do, so he's sitting on it. They're running out of money, it looks good. They've got a new public interest law firm that is funded by the Christian right, and they're reinvigorated. There's been an unexpected turn and it will cost us another $25,000."

Then, in the middle of the mayoral campaign, the city got a break. The preachers suddenly and mysteriously offered to go to mediation.

One May morning, about two weeks after the election and a month before I was to be sworn in, David Taub and I traveled to Charleston to meet with our lawyers and the principals from among the preachers and a new lawyer representing the preachers, Curtis Bostick, a reasonable-sounding fellow who appeared to know what mediation was all about. Reverend Baker was there too, even though by a legal maneuver he had by then been formally removed from among the list of plaintiffs.

The talking took the better part of the day. There was a lot of heat, but just enough light. At the end of the day, both sides had agreed to a new, and hopefully less arbitrary, city noise ordinance that would be based on a decibel reading. The city's insurer agreed to pay a modest amount (that I am not at liberty to reveal) to help pay some of the attorneys the preachers owed, and we were most of the way down the road. There were two blanks on the agreement: the decibel meter reading and the distance from the source of the noise from which the decibel reading should be taken. It was just a matter of the mediator coming to Beaufort and exercising his good judgment with respect to what decibel reading would constitute too loud and from what distance that reading should be taken. By agreeing to the mediated settlement, the city agreed to fashion its new noise law in accordance with the mediator's recommendations. Also under the terms of the settlement we couldn't say anything to the press, so we just waited for the mediator to come to Beaufort for a street preaching demonstration after which he would make his determination, and that would be that.

Two months later, after the mediator had rendered his findings, Council passed the new ordinance and after nine years of litigation, Bay Street was again a peaceful place for shopkeepers to conduct business.

As the reader will note, I had done very little—except to stay out of the way—in getting the street preacher case settled. But in public office, the credit and the blame are assigned whether you are directly involved or bonefishing in the Bahamas. The public knows very little of what exactly you did. It is the results that interest them. If you are in charge, unless you are very facile, you will be held responsible for the results.

But this I know: If I have anything to do with it, it will be a very long time before the City of Beaufort gets involved in a controversy the outcome of which tests constitutional principles like freedom of speech or religion. We'll leave that to bigger cities with deeper pockets.

The week following the resolution of the street preacher case, the city faced a trial date in a separate and unrelated case. As late as the 1980s, Beaufort County could have been described as a rural county with a handful of little towns scattered through it. That is no longer the case. In the '80s and '90s, Beaufort and the Sea Islands were increasingly discovered so that during that period the county's population nearly doubled from about 75,000 to over 130,000. The towns grew too, both in terms of population and area. When I came on Council in 1993, for example, Beaufort was a town of 5,520 acres. By 2003 it had grown to 12,735 acres. The city's budget grew from $4.8 million to $11.5 million over the same period.

As the city's land mass increased, its fire service coverage area increased as well. This caused the fire service areas of the surrounding rural fire districts to decrease by like amounts. The decrease in their service areas meant fewer properties for these independent fire districts to tax as they sought to deliver the fire protection they were charged with providing.

There's a provision in the Federal Home Loan Bank (FMHA) lending regulations that says if a governmental entity takes out an FMHA loan, it is illegal for any other governmental entity to disrupt the revenue flow that will repay the loan. The fire district on Beaufort's western boundary, the Burton Fire District, had such a loan, and the growth of Beaufort into their service area had arguably placed into jeopardy the revenues that would repay the loan. So in 1992 the Burton Fire District filed a lawsuit against Beaufort seeking compensation for the lost revenue.

After years of delay the judge finally demanded to hear arguments, setting the trial date for the day after Labor Day in 1999. I had been mayor for about ten weeks. I said to Bill Harvey: "Let's invite them to sit down and try to settle this thing. How about ten o'clock in the morning on Labor Day?" My thinking was if both sides gave up their holiday, that in itself would show resolve. Moreover, Labor Day was the day when there could be no more continuances. We were, in effect, on the courthouse steps.

I had met several times for lunch with the chairman of the Burton Fire District Commissioners, Gary Bright. He was a guy who had come up through the ranks, and he had a really good grasp of the problem. He wasn't obsessed with service territory and power, he just wanted to protect people's lives, homes, and property, and he thought his fire department should be paid fairly for doing so. We agreed on both those things, and we liked one another. That background made it easier in the negotiating room on Labor Day morning.

Since my side had called the meeting, I made the opening statement, one with perhaps a little New York bluster in it: "If we're here to protect fiefdoms," I said, "let's go home right now to our families and enjoy the holiday. But if we're here to protect the taxpayers' lives and homes and property, which is why I'm here, then I think we can work this thing out. Because then we're just talking about money, and the money people here can project revenues and put costs on things and we can reach an understanding of one another's needs. And that's the basis I propose we proceed on: what we each need, not what we want. If there are going to be any windfalls, they're going to have to come from the judge tomorrow. And I don't mind that. We'll pay what he tells us to pay and when the city's taxpayers tell me it's too much, I'll say, 'Don't tell it to me, tell it to the judge.' To me that's far preferable than having to say to them, 'Yeah, sorry, in retrospect it was too rich a settlement.' The taxpayers are very smart. They'll know fair when they see it, so if you're willing to proceed on that basis, let's see if we can find a solution that's fair to the people we each represent."

There were two topics of discussion throughout the day. The first was if Burton was going to respond to calls inside the city limits, which calls would they respond to; and likewise if the city was going to respond to calls not within the city, then calls from where? It rapidly became clear what we would be talking about was an "automatic aid" agreement, which simply says in these places this or that company responds. And in these areas where there's a question who can get there first, they both go and whoever gets to the scene first runs the scene. That means the two fire companies race to beat each other to scenes along the borders, which is good for the person who needs emergency assistance.

The other issue was classic arm wrestling, little different from buying a car on a car lot. Here's what we can do, and here's why we can't do more. Well, here's what we've got to have and here's why we've got to have it . . . all day long with forty-five minutes off for a late lunch.

At the end of the day we had a deal, a deal we were both proud to announce: the automatic aid agreement, plus Beaufort would compensate Burton for some of its lost revenue.

The City of Beaufort shares a border with the municipality to its immediate south, the Town of Port Royal. Port Royal had also been growing into the Burton Fire District's service territory. Accordingly, Burton had a similar lawsuit filed against Port Royal, just for smaller stakes. The next morning, literally on the courthouse steps, Port Royal and Burton settled their differences, using the Beaufort-Burton arrangement as their model. There were headlines enough to go around that day.

The Town of Port Royal and the City of Beaufort also had several other lawsuits at that time pending against each other. Being so close geographically, as the two had grown south and west into Burton or to the east on to Lady's Island, they had gotten tangled up trying to include within their boundaries commercial property owners who wished to come into one municipality or the other.

As two of the oldest municipalities on the eastern seaboard, the cities of Beaufort and Port Royal go back a long way together. And they have had their ups and downs.

Port Royal, featuring a first-class natural harbor, is arguably the site of the first Spanish settlement in America.

Situated on a magnificent bend of the Beaufort River a couple of miles up the river from Port Royal's harbor, and with a little ocean breeze that before air conditioning was worth millions, Beaufort came into its own in the late eighteenth and early nineteenth centuries as cotton became king. With the increasing profitability of Sea Island longstem cotton, the wives of the planters, quite justifiably hankering for both a little society and some relief from the steaming summer heat and mosquitos and malaria on the plantations, convinced their husbands they needed summer places in breezy Beaufort. Beaufort came to enjoy a significant expansion in those years as these families brought the luxuries of their plantation houses with them to town. Beaufort even enjoys its own vernacular architecture, as a result of these families' care for their comfort and prestige. The Beaufort style was developed through and was adapted to the various American architectural fashions from Federal in the 1780s through Greek Revival in the 1850s. At its essence the Beaufort style is five architectural elements, each of which is intended to keep the house cool in the summer heat by capturing the sacred breezes.

The war changed all that, of course. When Beaufort was captured and held by the Federal Navy in 1861, it marked the end of Beaufort as a summer resort for planters, and for the next hundred years, Beaufort and Port Royal struggled along with good humor and great dignity on shrimping, oystering, truck farming, and the services that can profitably be provided supporting the missions of military installations. Then, in the 1960s, Hilton Head Island, a forty-five-minute drive from Beaufort and Port Royal, began to emerge as a resort mecca for the well-heeled. The construction of the beachfront hotels and mansions on Hilton Head Island not only provided thousands of new jobs, but it re-introduced into the county rich people seeking comfort, prestige, and the society of their peers. Real estate values in Port Royal and Beaufort rose in the reflected glow of the new money being introduced into the county. Parcel by parcel, the two municipalities began to expand their boundaries so that by the 1970s they found themselves butting up one against the other, and growing out into the unincorporated sections of the county.

There were some rough spots, as for example when in the mid-'80s Beaufort Mayor Henry Chambers summarily announced that Beaufort, then a city of about 9,500, would "take over" Port Royal, then a town of about 3,500, thus infuriating Port Royal's leadership. And there were some successes, as for example when in 1995 Port Royal entered into a contract with Beaufort to supply fire protection to Port Royal, a service-sharing step that has served the interests of both communities.

On the Port Royal Town Council for over twenty years and an institution in the Town of Port Royal is a little dynamo of a lady named Yvonne Butler. Yvonne is the daughter of a Marine, and she's married to a Marine. Spunky, straight-laced, and direct, as she would tell you herself: "I call 'em exactly like I see 'em."

Yvonne knew the two towns shouldn't be litigating against each other, and I agreed with her, although we had never spoken with each other about it. I'd only met her once or twice. To meet Yvonne Butler once, however, is to have cause to remember her. We were probably both in the minorities on our councils at the time on this issue. She called me up one afternoon and invited me over to her house for a cup of coffee the next Saturday morning. She didn't say why, and I didn't ask. We sat at her kitchen table and chatted for a few minutes while I wondered what was on her mind. One of her granddaughters sat on a couch nearby doing her homework. Every once in a while our discussion was happily interrupted by a "Grandma, is six times nine fifty-four or fifty-six?"

It wasn't long until Yvonne got to the point. "It's not right for Port Royal and Beaufort to be fighting," she began. "We have great opportunities to be growing these cities, which is what we ought to be doing, opportunities that may not be there for long. And instead we're spending our precious time and resources squabbling amongst ourselves."

I said: "I'm with you 100 percent. If you and I work together, we can settle our differences. It's really pretty simple. Here's what let's do. You get a map and I'll get a map and we'll get together with our councils and managers and figure out where we have the opportunities to grow our towns. We'll each draw that on our map. Then you and I will get back together and see where the disputed areas are and whether there isn't some way to swap those around to where we can live with it."

It took a couple of months and a handful of meetings between representatives of the two towns. In the end, Beaufort gave up parts of Shell Point and Burton in exchange for an undivided interest in Lady's Island. In September the two town councils met in a joint session to, in effect, sign the peace treaty. I'd been mayor for about three months. With great ceremony, maps and documents and pens were passed around among the principals for their signatures. Lawyers fluttered around like butterflies. There were speeches of conciliation and congratulation. Had not there been so many Baptists among us, there probably would have been toasts too.

A few weeks after that I was on WJWJ-TV's public affairs call-in show, *Coastline*. A lady called in and said, "I live in Port Royal.

Now that you and Port Royal have made up, why don't you merge?"

I said: "I don't see political consolidation happening in our lifetimes. Each town has its own identity, and that's a good thing. But there are services that we could deliver together. There may be ways of enjoying economies of scale without losing autonomy. You know about fire protection, and I think both towns agree that's working. We should work on more things like that. Garbage collection comes to mind. When our recycling contracts come up, we ought to rebid them together and see if we can get a better per-customer deal."

There are talents and skills that you have that your predecessor did not, and there are talents and skills that your predecessor had that you do not. Because there are things you can do that your predecessor couldn't or wouldn't, if they're in the city's interests, do them while you can. Early successes are sweet because they show you and your constituents that you can do the job. To keep the job, however, you must convey you're just getting started.

At its extreme, this is the justification for term limits, although I do not personally believe term limits serve the taxpayers because where they have been made mandatory, good, reelectable, and experienced public officials find themselves required to step down. To me that creates an unnecessary brain drain.

If public officials aren't up to snuff, just throw them out.

13. Find the Capitals

HOW does the Billie Holliday song go? "Money you've got lots of friends crowding round your door."

Even in lean years there is a lot of loose change lying around unclaimed in both your state capital and in Washington. Most towns' entire operating budgets are chump change in their state capitals. Washington is on a scale of its own. But you can't get the money unless you go there.

It is amazing how few mayors and council-members go regularly to Washington. They go more often to their state capitals, but usually just to testify on bills. Too rarely do most meet with their legislative delegations, which is where the money is.

If you have money, you can make things happen. If you don't, it's a lot harder. The most beloved New York mayors in the twentieth century have been the ones who served when the economy was hot. LaGuardia, Wagner, and Koch were the three-termers. Each had the good fortune to face reelection when the city's economy was booming. Conversely, the one-termers, Impelliteri, Beame, and Dinkins, all faced reelection when the city's economy was slumping.

Your popularity will be affected by whether the town has discretionary income during your tenure. Of course it is important how the city's local revenue sources hold up. You have little control over that. But there's always "new" money in the capital for those who know how to get it. Here's how they do it.

The structure in both your state capital and in Washington is essentially the same. In both places there are delegations. These are the representatives and senators who are elected from your town and county. Meet with them.

Let's take your state capital first. Your town is probably represented by one or two state representatives and by perhaps a state senator or two. In the whole county there may be two or three senators and a half dozen or so state representatives. These elected officials have a loose association that is generally called a legislative delegation. If there were a Windswept County, Oklahoma, there would be a Windswept County legislative delegation. Each of the legislators who represent Windswept County in the state House and Senate sits on a couple of committees of the House or Senate. One or another of them is probably on many or most of the committees of the House and Senate. Thus, if you work with the whole group, there's a pretty good chance you can get the inside line on the activities of any committee in which you may have an interest.

Here's what you do. With your city manager, council-members, and department heads, get up a list of projects that will benefit your town, but for which you have no money in the town budget. Schedule a trip to your state capital and, in advance, request to meet with the members of the county delegation, making your request to the state senator who represents your town. If, for whatever reason, you don't get along with her, work through the state representative. (If you don't get along with her either, it's time to mend fences.)

Generally these elected officials will send high-level staffers to the meeting, people who know where the various pots of money reside and the criterion for each. For your part, go with a list of projects you need funded—now's your time to go through it. Start at the top and begin describing the projects. The more you know about the specifics of each project the better able you'll be to characterize it in different ways, ways that may fit the criterion for one or another funding source. It may be you'll want your city manager there too because he knows about the various aspects of each project too.

Keep notes, or make sure the city manager does. When there's hope for getting a project to fit the criterion for a funding source, write down the name of the staffer who has expressed hope and the funding source that came to their mind. After the meeting, follow up with that staffer to make sure you understand the strategy and timetable. Then, once you've got the timetable, go home and make sure you arrange to get the appropriate council action within the time frame so that your city can be positioned to get the money. Work through your local representative and senator to make sure they're tracking the progress of the request.

When your senator calls you up to tell you you've gotten the money, after thanking him, say, "When can you be here for a press conference to announce this?" Invite everyone who helped. When the project's completed, have a ribbon cutting and invite them all again.

If you do this, if you share the credit, they will help you the next time.

In 1998, the year before I ran for mayor, State Senator Holly Cork was about to retire. She represented Beaufort. The city had recently completed its greenways study, and I went up to Columbia to meet with Holly and others to talk about where some greenway money might be found. Beaufort's greenways study described a series of walking and biking trails that could be constructed throughout the city. She kindly took me over to Phil

Leventis's office, the third ranking state senator with a prominent place on the Finance Committee. We sat and talked and he said he would get $100,000 a year for three years to help build Beaufort's greenways. Holly must have known Leventis wanted to run for statewide office one day, but I didn't. So I was perplexed as to why this guy from upstate wanted to help us. I followed the meeting up with a letter that thanked him for seeing me and wished him the best with the $100,000 a year over three years plan that we had discussed. I offered to help in any way I could.

Holly left as planned and I apprised her successor, Scott Richardson, of the situation. The first year, sure enough, we got $100,000 in state dollars for our greenway. I called Senators Leventis and Richardson and Representative Edie Rodgers to set up a press conference in front of where the path would be built. I waited for the second and third installments, but they never came. Scott didn't have the seniority to deliver it, and Leventis quit the Senate to run unsuccessfully for lieutenant governor.

The section of the greenway we had chosen to be improved with the state money was a walking path to be installed across the Woods Bridge, the erector-set-style swing-span bridge that connects Beaufort to the islands. We found the rest of the money we needed back home by splitting the rest of the need with Beaufort County. The county agreed to split the cost of the balance with the city in exchange for the city dropping a lawsuit against them. When the time came to cut the ribbon, we invited everyone: city, county, state, and federal. But the best part is that now whenever I drive over the bridge, there are people walking or jogging along that section of the greenway.

This is how things get done. You have your list of needs and you go to your state capitol and to Washington to get them funded. If I hadn't gone to Columbia and Holly hadn't put me in touch with Phil Leventis, the project would probably still be on the drawing board. The first money is the hardest to raise. Then the "shovel in the ground effect" kicks in. Once government begins raising money for something or begins building something, the project develops momentum, because turning back would mean admitting error and/or conspicuously wasting tax dollars, and both of those are things that elected officials will go to great lengths to avoid the appearance of doing.

As Phil Leventis prepared his campaign for lieutenant governor in 2002, he called me up for a contribution. I was grateful to him that he'd gotten us the $100,000 "seed" money, but disappointed that the second and third installments had gotten lost in the shuffle. Following my "tit for tat" maxim, I gave him about a third of what he thought I should give—which was 100 percent more than I would have given him had he done nothing for the city.

14. Illusion

FOR us all there are what amount to two lives: the person who runs city hall and the person who gets out among his constituents. We are both people.

Honey Fitz, the legendary mayor of Boston in the early 1900s, was known for his beautiful singing voice. Hugh Carey, the governor of New York in the 1970s, would sing his way out too. He couldn't sing, but the Irish playfulness with which he tried always brought smiles to the lips of the crowd. Bill Cork, father of Holly Cork, a state senator who represented Hilton Head Island in the 1980s, used to conclude his campaign appearances by playing the spoons. Franklin Roosevelt had his cigarette holder, Churchill his cigar. After a riverside bill signing, Massachusetts Governor Bill Weld jumped into the Charles River in his business suit and tie and shoes to demonstrate that the river had been cleaned up.

These antics aren't for everyone, but for those who can pull off such performances, they're gold. Why? The electorate wants to know who you are. Antics such as these make it easy for them. The electorate wants to know that you are one of them and you are there for them. When they regard you favorably, it's because they think, "He's doing what I would be doing, if I was there." It's a fantasy on the part of the electorate, but one that is helpful to the elected.

Slogans serve the same purpose. Huey Long patented "Every man a king." Ed Koch made "How'm I doin'?" famous.

Lee Atwater coined the saying "perception is reality," and that concept is now universally accepted. One of my favorites in this genre is "the secret." This is a Bronx trick, one of many from where politics is played as hard as anywhere else in the U.S.A. Victor Botnick in the Koch City Hall was a master of this move, as was Stanley Friedman. The young political pup wants to show the crowd he's a player, so at the big political dinner, when all eyes are on the biggest shot politician in the room, the pup goes up to the man and whispers something banal in his ear: "Lois looks great," or "I'll keep an eye on the car." The big-shot politician responds, instinctively also in a whisper, "Thanks." The pup, again cupping his hands and whispering through them into the big shot's ear, says: "Sure thing, anytime. Call me. Frankie Smilowicz. I'm in the book." Then he gives the big shot an easily observed knowing look and walks away from him.

When Frankie gets back with his friends, they all want to know what the man said, and what Frankie said to the man. Of course Frankie can't say. It's between him and the man. The next day Frankie's supervisor looks at Frankie a little differently because now he knows Frankie knows the man. Perception is reality.

From time to time I've heard Capitol Hill staffers say things like: "The guy's unbelievable, in Washington there's no one smarter—he knows the rules inside out and he picks up legislative nuances like a vacuum cleaner. I couldn't believe it when I saw him at the Watermelon Festival in Pineville, and there he was oinking like a pig."

That's just a good politician.

Washington staffers often see just the legislative side of what their bosses do. It's left to a couple of trusty old buddies back in the district to take care of the "public" side. But the public side gets you elected, and you have to get elected and stay elected to get the things done that you came to do. I'm not just talking about congressmen, although their cases stand out in the greatest relief because of the distances between Capitol Hill and some of the districts. For mayors and councilmen or selectmen, there's no distance at all. Ed Koch used to say: "It'll cost you seventy-five dollars to take the shuttle down to Washington to picket the president. It'll cost you $60 to go to Albany to picket the governor. But you can picket me for the price of a subway token. It's only sixty cents, so come on down."

Besides oinking like a pig at the Watermelon Festival, there are some things that elected officials should do to keep their faces and views well known by the electorate. Incumbency has its privileges. What follows are some of those privileges and how you can use them to shape public opinion and keep yourself visible.

No one can do all these things all the time. There aren't enough hours in the day. But everyone who wants to do the job and keep the job should pick from this list regularly.

If you can express yourself on paper, then you should write several op-ed pieces for the local newspaper each year. If you can't write well, you should get someone who can to help you put such pieces together. Failing that, get a tape recorder and explain the issues to the microphone. Then, using a computer with grammar- and spellcheck-equipped software, transcribe the tape. Heed the computer's grammar and spelling suggestions, and read your first hundred or so words with particular care. It may take you a little while to get warmed up and your "lead" is a paragraph or two down into the piece. Show what you've got to a supporter or two and listen carefully to their suggestions. When you've gotten the piece where you want it (editors generally like four hundred to six hundred words), call the newspaper and tell the editor the piece is coming.

Use pieces like this to explain why you are going to vote one way or another on an upcoming issue of importance to the community. But once you get into the groove, understand that you don't have to limit your topics to matters coming before council. If a community leader whom you knew well just died, write a tribute to her. If there's a local milestone coming up, put together a piece on why it is still relevant to the community. If the federal government or the state government is passing out unfunded mandates at a quicker-than-usual pace, get the city manager or one of the city staffers to put together a first draft containing the details, then finish it off with some hot rhetoric of your own. If the hospital is trying to expand, be its advocate. If the schools are struggling to keep up with the technological revolution, cheer them on.

By getting elected, you have shown that you understand who your political base is. The op-ed piece is one of the ways you communicate with your base. Its great advantage is that you write all the words, and your words are not subjected to the digestion and regurgitation of the news-gathering process.

There is a theory of campaigning that goes like this. You kick off your campaign among your closest supporters by activating your base. Then, in the middle of the campaign, you reach out to undecided groups in an effort to win their support. And finally, at the end of the campaign, you "come home" to your base.

Choose your op-ed topics using a similar approach. In your first few months in office write about topics that are of particular interest to your base. Then begin to scatter your topics around with an eye toward appealing to some of the groups that supported your opponent. Then, in the months before the next election, come home to your base. Meanwhile, create a campaign Web site and post all your op-ed pieces there.

There may be weekly or biweekly newspapers in your market. Here's how to include them and get a bigger bang for your op-ed buck. Let's say the African-American weekly comes out on Wednesdays. And let's say one of your op-ed pieces would be of interest to the general audience that reads the daily and particularly to the readers of the African-American weekly. You call the editor of the weekly the week before and ask him to reserve you some space on his op-ed (opposite the editorial) page. Then write the piece, getting it to the weekly on Monday, so it can be included in Wednesday's issue. Also on Monday, you write "embargoed until Thursday, June 5" in big letters on the top and bottom of the piece and fax it to the daily paper. Then call the editor to make sure she got the piece and noted the embargo. This has the effect of giving the weekly a day's head start on the publication of the piece, which is an advantage they rarely get and very much appreciate. Yet it keeps things simple for the daily's editors who, if they cared enough about your piece to want to run it the day after it appeared in the weekly, would otherwise be scrambling around on Wednesday afternoon (after someone noticed your piece in the weekly), trying to get your permission to rerun your piece and remaking their op-ed page to fit it in. This way everybody gets something.

Akin to the op-ed is the letter to the editor. Letters should be used by elected officials to correct false statements by others, especially in the newspaper in question. Don't be shy about firing off a letter now and then to keep the record straight. Make letters as short as possible and front-load them. As in a news story, tell the reader right at the top what the letter's about, then follow with all the reasons why what you've told them is so is in fact so.

When you have been misquoted in a news story so badly that your position is not recognizable, demand a correction. Don't be shy about this, either. If the newspaper's misquoted you on the front page, then that's where the correction should appear.

The TV chat show appearance is also a powerful tool in the incumbent's toolbox. There are a couple of things to know. First, be cool and understated. Remember the TV camera is right in your face and you are right in the faces of your viewers. So go easy on them. A little gentle humor is always welcome, and tenseness and nervousness are to be avoided. The pros all say, "Never look at the camera." I'm going to offer one exception to their rule: Look into the camera when you deliver the punch line.

If you're out in the community, as you should be, then you're going to pick up stories. Make a couple of these your standard openings for speeches. If people end up hearing them more than once, if the stories are humorous, it's all right. Here's one of Ed's that I can repeat word-for-word twenty years later: "When I was running for mayor I was at a senior center in the Bronx. I was taking questions and a woman says, 'Mr. Koch, what are you going to do about crime?' I say, 'Well, it's the judges. They have to be tougher. You know there was one judge recently who got mugged and you know what he said? He said, "This mugging of me will in no way affect my decisions in matters of this kind." ' And a little lady stands up in the back of the room and she says, 'Well, then mug him again!' "

To get the maximum punch out of that story in a TV studio, I would suggest that Ed turn to the camera with a twinkle in his eye but without breaking his cadence just when he said, ". . . and she says, 'Well, then mug him again.' "

When you're going on a half-hour, one-on-one interview show, consider in advance what you want to talk about. The time's going to go very quickly, so you want to use it well. Generally the interviewer will tell you before the cameras roll the general areas of discussion she wants to get into. You can suggest a couple of your own at that time and she may put yours on her list. But don't rely on that.

A better approach is to write your six points or so down on an index card and hold it in your palm. When she's speaking her question into the camera (the camera with the red light on is the one that's going out over the air), you look at your card and figure out how you're going to twist the question around so that you give the answer you want. The classic exchange in the twist-the-question genre goes something like this:

> **Question:** "Mr. Mayor, you've had a rough time with the budget this year. It seems everything's gone wrong for you from the copy shop to the police department. Do you still think you'll have to lay off police officers? And if so, how many?"

> **Answer:** "Well, Phoebe, getting the budget passed will be tough right up to the end, but we'll do it. The really important thing to watch will be 'Can we get it balanced without a tax increase?' You know there are always pressures to raise taxes. Some of my colleagues will say we have to. The big-spenders are setting that up now. Don't believe them. People are paying enough. Sometimes even government has to live within its means . . ."

Watch how the Washington pols try to pull this trick on Tim Russert on Sunday mornings, and how he tries to pull them back to where they don't want to be.

Wear something that doesn't distract people. A little polka

dot, shimmer, or a too-short skirt can turn out to be more interesting to the viewer than your message.

Be polite, but stand your ground. After you get comfortable, you'll find that you're in control of the show when talking about what you want to talk about. Mix humor with pathos. When you're on your game, it's like batting practice: the interviewer is throwing you balls and you are hitting them all over the park.

But things can go bad fast. Beware of microphones, even when the technicians say they're off. Don't say anything anywhere near any microphone that you wouldn't want to see on the front page of the next day's paper. President Bush and Vice President Cheney relearned this one in their 2000 campaign the hard way. But they slipped out of the noose. Others haven't been so lucky.

Give speeches when you are invited to the Rotarians and the Kiwanians and the other community groups. Speeches are like op-eds. Think in advance about what you want to say. But don't read a speech. Speak from notes written by you on index cards. Most important, practice the speech once or twice at home. Open with one of those favorite stories from around town, something light. Keep the substance of your remarks short so you can take questions at the end. If you know your stuff, the questions will be the fun part anyway. Don't worry about being critical of others in public life, but try not to use their names.

Here's a Lee Atwater trick that's worth trying if you've got an energized group of core supporters and election day's approaching. Nothing looks better on TV than you with 150 Kiwanians standing and cheering you. But how do you get them out of their seats? First, write a speech that builds up to and then ends with your announcing something that's news and that the community wants, say a new football stadium for the high school or a new parking facility downtown. You don't have to say you've got the money, just that you favor the new project and you'll work to make it happen. Practice the speech until you know it's good. Then make sure the TV camera crews are in the back of the room. Tell them there'll be news in your speech that they won't want to miss, but don't tell them what it is or they may not come to find out. Get as many of your people into the room as you can, but—this is the Atwater part—position ten or twelve of your most reliable supporters throughout the room as if you're the batter and they're the fielders in a baseball game, with a "pitcher" at front row center. Cue your team, especially the pitcher, to the applause line at the end of the speech, telling them, "When I get to the applause line, get up and start clapping hard as soon as the pitcher gets up." It will amaze you to see all the other Kiwanians rising with them. And the footage of the crowd standing and clapping as you humbly sit down after concluding your remarks will be irresistible to the editors back at the TV stations' cutting rooms.

There will also be opportunities to march in parades and cut ribbons. Seize them, as many as you can manage. If you get heckled, stick your thumbs in the air and imagine they're cheering you. It comes with the territory. The hecklers are probably zealots anyway, which is why you should not engage them. It's not the heckling that counts, it's how you react to it.

I prefer walking in parades to riding in the back seat of a convertible because you can control the pace of things better, and when the parade comes to a temporary halt you can go over to the curb and touch people.

In politicking there's an absolute magic to touching. Old timers know that "pressing the flesh" translates directly into votes.

One day in the Koch City Hall, Queens Borough President Donald Manes really needed Ed's vote at the Board of Estimate. Donny came to Ed's office immediately before the vote. I was there and I watched the whole thing. Donny pitched Ed on what he needed and all the reasons why he needed it and he didn't let Ed get a word in edgewise. Then, without taking a breath, he said it was time to go up to the Board of Estimate chambers to vote. It's amazing they made it up the stairs without falling. Manes was about five-foot-ten and 250 pounds; Ed's about six-foot-two and 230 pounds. Donny had Ed around the waist with his left arm and he was squeezing him hip-to-hip. With his right arm he had reached behind his own left shoulder and he had Ed by the neck. And somehow he had gotten his left leg in between Ed's legs and had hooked it around Ed's right shin so that they were in lock-step. There was no getting away from him. Ed's vote was assured.

Physical contact equals votes. Where except at a parade do you get that many of your constituents together in one place, especially all standing in a line? What a great opportunity to touch people.

When Pope John Paul II first came to New York in 1979, the Vatican's advance man, Bishop Marshenkas, declared in the advance meetings that no politicians could be in His Holiness's motorcade. So my job as Mayor Koch's advance man was to make sure Ed was at every appropriate event to greet the Pope, that he stayed there to say good-bye to the Pope, and then to have Ed standing at curbside when the Pope's glass-enclosed "Popemobile" came to a stop at the next event, and that Ed stayed at that event so that he could escort the Pope to his Popemobile and bid him farewell, and then that Ed was there to greet the Pope at the event following that, and so forth. It was a wonderful logistical challenge. My tools were all the boats and helicopters and motorcycle cops I needed. Ed choppered over the Pope, he cruised by him in police boats, and he sped by him on side streets with motorcycle escorts. This went on in all of the boroughs except Staten Island.

On the second day of his visit, the Pope was scheduled to give an outdoor mass at Battery Park downtown and then proceed through the crowd-lined streets of Manhattan in his Popemobile up to St. Patrick's Cathedral in midtown. We expected the procession uptown to take about forty-five minutes. I had Ed's car and a half-dozen motorcycles standing by at Battery Park. Once Ed had seen the Pope off in his Popemobile, we screamed up the West Side to about Forty-eighth Street, then we cut east to Sixth Avenue to where the Pope's motorcade was expected to pass on its way to St. Patrick's Cathedral at Fiftieth and Fifth. My idea was that we'd walk from there along the thronged streets just ahead of the Pope, reaching St. Patrick's about the time the procession did.

I've never heard a politician get a better reception anywhere in the world. As we walked east on Fiftieth Street the crowd was practically clawing at Ed. You'd have thought he was Elvis back from the dead. People were calling out his name and weeping— Ed Koch was having transferred to him in part the affection and reverence the crowd felt for John Paul. While this is a dramatic example, the same is true in your hometown parade. Know who's well regarded and who's not, and stay away from the bums.

Make ribbon-cuttings fun too. You get to say about three lines right before you cut the ribbon. Everybody's excited. If what you say is halfway humorous, they'll laugh. Invite everybody to put their hands on yours to help you cut. My line, immediately after the ribbon's been cut, is always: "We're open for business!"

You will also be invited to various receptions. These are different from your cousin's Christmas party or your neighbor's cocktail party. Accordingly, you should behave differently. A reception is an opportunity for you to hear from the opinion-makers in your community. Don't wait for them to come up to you. Reach out to them. This means circulating around the room. Although it may at first feel as if you are being rude, "working a room" is an obligation of your office, and once you've got the hang of it, it can be done with efficiency and grace. If you do it well, you can see virtually everyone in the room, and still make it home for dinner.

Here's the secret. If you know the person you're about to greet, show that you do by greeting them by name. If you don't, introduce yourself. In either case, draw them out by talking about them. Don't overwhelm them with talk because what you really want is to hear from them. If you're asked a question, answer it fully, but don't say anything you don't want all over town.

Receptions are where you, in effect, take comments, complaints, and, if you're lucky, plaudits. They are also where you uncover hidden resources in your community. Leave pregnant pauses amid the small talk, enabling those you meet to speak to you seriously. This is when people will tell you of their interest in serving on this or that unpaid city committee, or for your reelection campaign. This is when you'll find out what people are saying about you or your fellow council-members or staffers. This is also when you'll pick up gossip on your adversaries.

When you've given someone ample opportunity to speak about the town or politics or whatever else your presence brought to their mind—or when they begin repeating themselves—move on gracefully. Helping to keep you moving is one of the many places where a good political spouse is invaluable.

Go anywhere there's a crowd. If the master of ceremonies

will introduce you, let yourself be introduced. If you're invited to speak, keep it to thirty seconds. To paraphrase FDR: "Be short, be funny, and be still." But don't agree to serve as the judge of anything. There are always more losers than winners, and the losers won't forget you.

Get out of the office and onto the street. When the staff says there's a problem at the Twelfth Street transfer station and the neighbors are complaining, your next words should be "I'll meet you there in fifteen minutes." Two things will happen. First, you'll see the problem for yourself, so you'll be more likely to understand it fully and solve it correctly the first time. And, just as important, when you get there and stand there with the staff analyzing the problem, at least a couple of the neighbors will see you and hurry over. That's good. If they're furious, let them vent. Listen carefully to them and indicate you understand their concern. But don't let them use ugly or profane language. Keep the meeting businesslike, and don't promise anything until you've got all the facts. If you don't know the neighbors you meet there, ask for their names, addresses, and telephone numbers and jot these down yourself. If you and the staff can solve the problem without a community meeting, then call the person who was most in your face and tell him what you're going to do. Don't leave this to the staff. Word will get around the neighborhood in an instant that it was you who showed up, you who cared, you who got the indolent staff motivated to solve the problem, and you who communicated the solution back to the neighborhood.

If a meeting's required to solve the problem, chair it. Make sure the appropriate representatives of the neighborhood and from the staff can be there. If representatives of other governments should be there, get them there. If people are still irate, hold the meeting at city hall. They'll behave better there. Open these kinds of meetings by stating the problem in broad terms. If you're not great with names, as I'm not, then at the outset ask everyone in the room to identify themselves and why they're there, beginning with yourself. Then turn the meeting over to the staff to state the details of the problem. Allow the neighbors to ask questions and make comments. Don't rush. Again, keep it businesslike and don't permit any profanity. (My line is: "If you're going to engage in profanity, I'm leaving." That usually ends it.)

Conclude the meeting by stating what the next step is. It's often a good idea to pass a piece of paper around the room for everyone to sign in. This will help you find the group for the next meeting. It will also go into your "friends file" back at your office. If the problem is solved satisfactorily, you might want to call on one or two of the meeting's participants in the next campaign.

If the problem can't be solved by election season, find a reason to stall. If the solution that you and the neighborhood both want costs more money than the city has handy, promise to take the matter up in the next city budget cycle and explain how the budget process works. Convey to the neighbors that you will be their advocate and invite them to come to the budget hearings so that they can personally tell the full council of the need.

Get to know whoever writes the editorials at the newspapers. Go to lunch with them several times a year whether you need an editorial that week or not. By getting to know them and by reading their editorials, you'll develop a feel for what kind of issues they like to opine upon. You can influence that too.

If you think the newspaper might run an editorial on an issue before your government, call up the editorial writer and express your point of view. Sometimes your call will prompt the writer to include your point of view. And sometimes you'll feel as if you wasted your time because no editorial appeared. You didn't. The opinion-makers read the editorial page. Access to its writers is one of the privileges and obligations of incumbency, even when it comes to nothing.

Get to know the reporters who cover you too. Know their children's names and where they go to school. While reporters are not your friends, there is a symbiotic relationship between politicians and press people: they must have one another. It follows then that it's a good thing to get to know these people that you need, and what's important to them, and whether they like their editors (usually they don't), and what their deadlines are, and what else is on their beat and so forth. All this information will come in handy. It should also be no surprise that reporters are also a very good source of news. They make it their business to know things like who's thinking of running for what, and who's thinking of not running for reelection, and who's angry with whom and why. And here again, these are things that come in handy.

As I noted earlier, no one can be all these places and do all these things. You will have to pick and choose. I suggest you pick and choose within each group, rather than excluding any one group altogether. But there's another consideration: your family, assuming you have one.

A good political spouse is hard to come by. As with reporters and movie stars, divorce rates among politicians aren't pretty. The hours are strange, the temptations are great, there are too many phone calls to make, and there are too many canceled vacations, weekends, and romantic dinners. Being mayor is not like running the local pack-and-ship shop. It takes a very self-confident person to be the spouse of a celebrity, and politicians are celebrities inside their districts. There's often a lot more being sacrificed in these relationships than the participants see or understand. If your spouse will come with you to events, you're lucky. The ones who enjoy it are one in a hundred.

In this respect single, childless people typically have a great advantage: more time. The disadvantage is your constituents want to know whether you're straight or gay. The answer is that it's none of their business. It's not like mayors or selectmen are guarding state secrets and some Christine Keeler or Anthony Blunt is going to seduce them in order to learn the secret garbage collection overtime figures.

If you have children, take the kids along once in awhile. Your constituents will want to see your family, even if it's not the perfect nuclear family. And kids love parades. Children who grow up around politics have a great advantage later in journalism, business, and, Heaven forbid, politics. The average American kid gets subjected to a lot worse than having to endure a rubber chicken dinner and a couple of political speeches once a month. Most important, sharing some of what you are with them will make you and your child closer.

In the end, all you can do is be yourself, and in the end that's all your constituents want you to be. They can smell a phony a mile away. And phonies don't get elected.

15. Principle

THE best political move Richard Nixon made as president was to go to China. If Jimmy Carter had tried the same thing, it would have been a disaster. It took an old cold warrior like Nixon to bury that hatchet.

In my six years as a city council-member, I was careful to be nonpartisan. I avoided party functions, which saved a lot of time too. Where I made campaign contributions or appearances, I tried to support candidates from both parties. My line was: "I know all these people. I work with them. I support people on the basis of whether they're good for Beaufort. I don't care whether they're Democrats or Republicans, so long as they're good for Beaufort."

The fact is that polling and television have sapped the traditional strength of the political parties. Polls tell candidates what the electorate wants, and commercials allow candidates to take their messages straight to the people, bypassing the traditional information disseminating role formerly performed by political organizations. The larger the town, the more this becomes true.

If a town is overwhelmingly Republican in general, a Democrat cannot win no matter how much TV time he buys. However, in such a town the big contest will be the Republican primary. And the winner of the Republican primary will be the candidate who best followed the route laid out by her polling results. In most towns that will include an advertising campaign with television ads.

Voters get a general impression of someone and they hold to it unless something big comes along to change it. In my case, since I had been associated with Ed Koch and New York, it was assumed that I was a Democrat even though on Council I had consistently voted to cut the budget wherever necessary to keep the property tax rate flat.

In June 1999, with the South Carolina presidential primary approaching in February 2000, the people who wanted to see Arizona Senator John McCain become the Republican party's presidential nominee were beginning to get organized. The campaign's national strategists had already determined that the senator would not actively participate in the Iowa caucuses, but would instead concentrate his efforts on the New Hampshire primary. Two weeks after New Hampshire came the South Carolina primary. McCain's people had identified New Hampshire and South Carolina as the first two essential steps toward his winning the nomination. Thus New Hampshire and South Carolina received from them an inordinate amount of attention.

I had been mayor for about two weeks when Richard Quinn, McCain's South Carolina media consultant, called to say the senator wanted to meet with me at my office. Quinn is a Columbia-based political consultant. It was at that moment that I perceived the importance of the upcoming primary. If Senator McCain was going to come meet me one-on-one at my office, he clearly intended to run a statewide grassroots-and-doorbells campaign. I pictured him standing on stoops and talking to voters who were wrapped in their bathrobes.

I said, "I'll meet with anyone who's seriously running for president."

Quinn said, "No commitments. He just wants to meet you and tell you what he's about."

"Fine," I said. "I'm looking forward to meeting him, and listening. Oh, there is one thing," I added. "I need a bridge."

Quinn said, "Tell him." And we set up the day and time.

At ten in the morning ten days later, John McCain and Richard Quinn walked into my office. The senator was shorter than I had expected. He exhibits a bantamweight's feisty demeanor. His neck is a little sturdier than is common, which adds to the impression that there are some muscles inside his starched white shirt. Although I hadn't read his book, I was somewhat familiar with his POW experiences, and there's something about a bona fide war hero that also tends to convey resolve and toughness. He came in fast, talked fast, and seemed to know just what he wanted, my endorsement, and that too led to the impression that this was a guy to be reckoned with.

At the time there were still a half-dozen or so Republicans in the primary, and with Bush the clear front-runner the question was, Would this be a race or a coronation? Several days earlier Ed Koch had been quoted as saying Senators McCain and Bradley are going to make the primary season interesting. They're the two to watch. Koch's comments gave McCain a lift, and sure enough, he did make it interesting for a while. My modest participation in the McCain campaign exactly corresponded with that period of time during which he was making it interesting.

Our meeting lasted about thirty minutes. We spent the first ten telling Koch war stories. That led the senator, who was very pleased by Ed's recent statements, into an account of why he was running: to shake up the pork barrel/special interests system that has disenfranchised the regular guy and works just for the special interests. There was passion in his voice, and you got the immediate impression that here was an honest guy out of the inner circle in Washington who was sincerely disgusted by how the system had jumped the tracks. His intensity was very appealing. It was Fighting Bob LaFollette and all that populism stuff you thought had happened a long time ago. It was also disarming for a guy who just wanted a bridge for his small town. As he was talking I was thinking: You know, Bill, you'd have a lot easier time getting your bridge off of either George W. Bush or Al Gore.

But a great politician can make you dream his dream, and John McCain's dream was a good dream. The way lobbyists influence the results of elections so as to feather the nests of their clients is wrong. So much waste and corruption flows from those relationships that the health of the country requires that that system of influence be changed. Here was a guy who was willing to make the fight, and it would be a withering one. A great politician can use words to create something from nothing, and that is what John McCain did in Beaufort that day.

I let him wind down, as is the custom in such situations, and as he was doing so I was thinking about all the veterans and military dependents in Beaufort. I was thinking how well he'd run in Beaufort, how he would probably even appeal to some Democrats, and that the retired military community in town would be for him with passion. Adding up the political equation in my mind, I concluded that while I would probably not get a bridge, being for McCain might very well be good for me anyway. But whether it was or not, McCain was what Washington needed.

It was my turn.

"I'm for you," I said. "I'm a soldier in your army. What do you want me to do to help?"

A big grin came over his face, and he just shined it on me for a few moments, as if no one had ever said they wanted him to be their next president before. (He was, after all, at 3 percent in the national polls and below even that in South Carolina.) Then he started up again: "I'll never make you anything but proud you supported me. I'm going to run a campaign that you, that your children, will be proud of. We're going to make the government . . . we're going to make the country . . . a better place." He stood up and shook my hand and thanked me again for my support, and he was out the door. As I watched him and Richard Quinn, who had said absolutely nothing except "hello" when he came in and "thank you" when he went out, walk down the little sidewalk outside my office, I thought, I don't have any idea what I'm supposed to do now. My guess is none of us had the slightest idea.

A couple of days later Quinn called just to confirm that I was still on board. I said, "I never mentioned the bridge."

He said, "I noticed that."

I said, "But I'm still going to need it."

Quinn said, "Well, there'll be a time for that."

I didn't hear anything more for several months. Then I read in the papers that Mark Sanford and Lindsey Graham were going to be McCain's statewide campaign chairmen. About Mark I wasn't surprised, but Lindsey Graham's support did catch my attention. He and Mark were good friends, and I had met him a few times at Mark's house. He has a winning sense of humor and a very engaging smile, but my perception was that he was way to the right of me, especially on things like abortion and school prayer. Since he represented the upcountry, the "Buckle of the Bible Belt," section of South Carolina, I knew his constituents must be more conservative than Sanford's, or mine. I had just figured he'd be for Bush.

When I saw Mark in Beaufort shortly afterward, I asked him how our man was doing. His reply surprised me. "I don't know," he said. That was about ninety days before the primary. McCain was ringing doorbells in New Hampshire, it appeared to me, and everyone else was just waiting to see what would happen there. Then, as things started looking more promising in New Hampshire, apparently, the campaign's managers began making their South Carolina plans.

About two weeks before the New Hampshire primary Richard Quinn called me. "We're scheduling the senator to be in Beaufort on February 3 and we'd like to have a breakfast at your house."

I said, "What kind of breakfast do you have in mind?"

He said, "Well you know, some community leaders, some friends, a chance for the senator to meet some of his key supporters in Beaufort County."

I was picturing a handful of local politicians and businessmen sitting around my dining room table drinking coffee and eating doughnuts.

I said, "Sure, have as many as you want." Two things were on my mind. First, it's a big old house, one that can easily handle one hundred to two hundred people inside. Second, my wife and I had recently split up, and she had taken the dining room table and chairs with her, and I hadn't gotten around to replacing them. If McCain had a few people, it seemed to me, my empty dining room would be obvious. But if there were a lot, it would look as if I'd moved the furniture out to make room for the crowd. "Just make sure the campaign sends me some advance people to get the coffee," I added.

Quinn said, "Oh yeah, sure, the campaign will take care of everything." And sure enough over the next several days, as the New Hampshire primary approached, advance people called up and came to look the place over.

On February 1 McCain stomped on George W. Bush in the New Hampshire primary. He beat him by eighteen points. I was home with my children when the results were announced from Concord. I was whooping and hollering and strutting around. My son, Henry, then fourteen, said: "What are you so excited about?"

I said, "My man just came in in New Hampshire. Yesterday he was nothing. Today he's leading the race!"

The next morning, the morning before the breakfast, the phone started ringing. South Carolina is a Republican stronghold. In 1988 Lee Atwater put this early "Gateway to the South" South Carolina primary in place as a way of making the state a player in presidential politics, and from his grave his magic was working. The political eyes of the nation were turning to the Palmetto State and to little Beaufort. The breakfast would be McCain's first appearance in South Carolina, and the press wanted to know all about it. All the callers wanted to know who's invited.

I said, "Everybody in town, Republicans and Democrats alike. We're not going to turn anybody away."

Through the day I could feel the excitement building. People I'd never met, some whose names I'd never heard, called up with their stories about how the senator had touched their lives. Could they come? I said, "Sure, and bring a friend."

Even though the temperatures were expected to be in the forties, we decided we'd better move the event outside. The senator would make his remarks from my front steps to the crowd that would be assembled in the front yard. The house would be the backdrop.

Late in the day I called Ed Koch in New York. "Ed," I said, "I'm having a McCain rally at my house tomorrow. I'm going to be introducing him. What do you think I should say?"

Ed said, "Well what do you want to say?"

"When I met with him last summer I was struck that he's a reformer, and he's a Republican. You know there aren't too many of those. Abraham Lincoln and Teddy Roosevelt come to mind. It's been awhile. Maybe this is his time."

Ed said, "Where are you calling from?"

I said, "Beaufort."

He said, "Well then you better not say anything about Lincoln."

I said, "I'm following you."

He said, "How about Reagan? I don't know why, but all those people [by which he meant Republicans] are nuts about Reagan."

I said, "Okay. I guess I'm okay on Reagan. But what did he reform?"

Ed paused for an instant. Then he said, "He reformed the Commies!"

We both howled with laughter.

When I got home from my office, semitrailer trucks had begun to arrive, and crews of carpenters and technicians worked through the night to put up risers for the dozens of cameras that would be traveling with the senator.

Having been one myself, I enjoyed watching the advance people do their work, although some of them were so green it was painful. But why shouldn't they have been? A month earlier there had been virtually no South Carolina campaign. Just Richard Quinn, Lindsey Graham, and Mark Sanford. A week before, as the polls gyrated in New Hampshire, no one in South Carolina had any idea whether McCain would reach South Carolina dead or alive.

The breakfast was called for eight o'clock on Thursday morning, February 3. At six the first guest arrived—Kenny Zentner, a local realtor, dressed in a suit. I pulled on some pants on the run to answer the door. Although we'd never met, naturally we struck up a conversation. Since that morning we've had several dozen conversations, always about traffic. Kenny Zentner is my traffic conscience: he hates traffic congestion, and every time he is in a backup he pulls out his cell phone.

"Mayor," he'll say. "I'm on Boundary Street and the traffic's creeping along. What's up?"

Kenny's primary purpose in arriving early was to get a good seat. I took him out front and showed him there were no seats, then I suggested he come back in an hour.

By 7:00 a.m. there were a hundred people in the yard. By 7:30 a.m. there was a line outside my front gate and up the block. At 8:00 a.m., when the senator was scheduled to arrive, well over a thousand people stood in my front yard.

My instructions from the McCain advance were that I was to meet the candidate's bus at Craven and Carteret Streets and walk him the two blocks down Craven Street to my house. In 1994, as a newly elected city councilman, I had spearheaded the effort to "get the buses off The Point." Now that effort was paying an additional dividend. These walk-and-talk images make good TV, and Craven Street, with its overhanging oak trees draped in Spanish moss, is very picturesque in a Southern gothic way. Our little walk would show off Beaufort well.

At about 8:45 a.m. the bus, the Straight Talk Express, as the campaign called it, pulled up and Senator McCain and his wife Cindy got off, all relaxed and cheerful, like a couple going to a football game. Lindsey was there too and together the four of us walked down Craven Street. It was one of those roller-derby walks where a half-dozen TV and still photographers are walking backwards up the street in front of you and shoving one another for position while they are filming your every gesture, and meanwhile dozens more are running past us to get set up down the street. But for all that we had a nice chat about his big win and I told them a little Beaufort history.

When we got to my front gate, the crush began. The yard was filled to capacity. The police estimated there were 2,000 people there. Of Beaufort's 13,000 residents, about 4,500 are registered voters, so it would be within the range of responsible hyperbole to say half the town was there.

When Jimmy Carter ran for reelection in 1980, Ed Koch walked across Eighty-sixth Street with Walter Mondale. As Koch's advance man, I played a minor role in setting up that stop. It was my first exposure to the electromagnetic energy that is in a presidential crowd. It's a very physical thing to be in the center of. Supporters reach over other supporters from four and five feet away to try to touch or shake the hand of the candidate. It's a crush and you find yourself leaning against the crowd just to keep a little room to work in. This is one of those times when it helps to be big. McCain had one petite advance lady whose job it was to lead him up my sidewalk. I don't know who chose her, but what he needed that morning was a nose tackle. But it didn't matter. He and Cindy were just chatting with whomever they found themselves next to as if they were at a cocktail party. My job wasn't to be pushing people away from them, but to introduce them around, so I was in no hurry. The city attorney was there. I said, "Senator, this is Bill Harvey, the city attorney."

McCain said, looking Bill in the eye and taking Bill's hand in both of his, "Hi Bill, it's my pleasure to meet you, and I'd like to introduce you to my wife Cindy."

Then Cindy turned her clear eyes and lovely smile on Bill and told him how lucky he was to live in such a beautiful town. Now Bill grew up in South Carolina politics because his grandfather represented Beaufort in the state senate for many years and his father was the lieutenant governor and highway commissioner who appeared in Chapter One. He's met hundreds of office-holders and office-seekers, Southern gentlemen of all descriptions. Later that day I ran into Bill who said to me, "I've never met a politician who seemed so kind." And that was exactly the way John McCain was that morning.

I wondered for a moment whether McCain had Reagan's magic calm, or whether he was just still in the warp between being a national contender and a regular guy trying gamely to come from behind.

It took us twenty minutes to work our way through the crowd. Finally we were on the steps and it was time for me to call the crowd to order. "Good Morning, Beaufort!" I bellowed into the microphone, Marine Corps–style. Then I pointed out some people in the crowd, people who don't come to political rallies: a surgeon, a bee keeper, the first woman to land a jet on the deck of an aircraft carrier. My point was this: here is an unusual candidate who finds support from new places, who has brought new people into the process, who has formed a new coalition. "And what is it about him that makes him so? He's a reformer. He's a Republican reformer, and there hasn't been one of those along in some time. He says he'll do to the special interests what Teddy Roosevelt, another Republican reformer, did to the trusts. We need that. He's a reformer in the Reagan tradition, a happy warrior. We need that."

After a few words from Lindsey, the senator began with some very sweet praise for me, which is always a good thing in front of the hometown crowd. He said: "You got a smart mayor here. He's a pretty prescient fellow. He was for me when I was at three percent. So if you want to know what's going to happen in six months, just ask Mayor Bill Rauch."

From there he moved into his stump speech. You knew he'd given it dozens of times in New Hampshire, but the message was a good one—about the special interests and their lobbyists, and the need for campaign finance reform—and the Beaufort crowd ate it up, hissing and groaning whenever the special interests were mentioned.

I stood down several steps when McCain got rolling and so did Lindsey. We were standing together when McCain got to the part about pork barrel projects. At that reference I turned to Lindsey and whispered: "It's okay with me to cut them out in everyone else's district. But not Beaufort's." Lindsey grinned with a smile that said, No one will ever get the pork out of Washington. With that encouragement I said to him, "We need a bridge." To my amazement his face lit up. You could tell it was exactly what he wanted to hear. I hadn't known then, as I hadn't with Phil Leventis in Columbia, that Lindsey was looking to move up. Strom Thurmond had said he would be giving up his senate seat in 2002, and Lindsey was eyeing it. Out of the side of his mouth and with a glint in his eye he said, "Come to Washington." I did not forget the invitation.

After Senator McCain spoke and took a few questions, he worked his way back through the crowd and over to a microphone that had been set up right in front of the TV risers. While he was fielding questions from the press corps, I happened to see a friend of mine, Elayne Scott, whom you will recall from her participation in the controversy surrounding the widening of Highway 21 on St. Helena Island. If there is someone who is to the left of Elayne Scott and they live in Beaufort County, I don't know who it is. Elayne was at the McCain rally. As I said, we are friends, so I goaded her a little, saying, "Elayne, I wouldn't have expected to see you here at this Republican function."

She said: "Are you kidding? He's the only one of the bunch who's any good. It's a rotten system and he's the only one who's going to try to change it." She was right. That was why I was there too.

Several times in the next few weeks I was told that the breakfast stop in Beaufort was the best South Carolina stop McCain made. Several things give credence to that view. The first is that while McCain was having breakfast in Beaufort, his campaign higher-ups, cocky from New Hampshire, were meeting with Richard Quinn in Columbia and beginning to seize from Quinn day-to-day control of the South Carolina primary campaign.

It wasn't just McCain's national people who wanted Quinn off the Straight Talk Express, it was Bush's people too. In addition to running a political consulting and communications business, Quinn had also done some publishing. For a number of years he had edited *Southern Partisan*, a quarterly magazine that focuses on Southern history and heritage. Even though Quinn had resigned his position as editor of the magazine several years before the presidential primary, the Bush opposition research people combed through fifteen years of back issues of the magazine and compiled quotes from dozens of the magazine's writers. Where there had been anything published, in or out of context, that could possibly be construed as racially insensitive, they collected it.

With the researchers' materials in hand, the campaign operatives went to work on it. Several quotes were embellished with slight changes in wording to make them sound more provocative, including one quote from Reid Buckley that was cleverly stripped from context so that its meaning was actually reversed. After adding their own emphasis and hyperbole and attributing all the quotes from all the writers to Quinn, they circulated the dossier to the national press.

Suddenly Quinn himself was an issue in the campaign. Instead of the campaign's chief South Carolina strategist being able to devote his full energies to the campaign's day-to-day operations, now, just as the full campaign was moving into South Carolina, Quinn had to spend significant portions of his time chasing down old magazine stories, and giving interviews to reporters to show them what had been done and why it didn't at all mean he was a racist. Another costly result of the turmoil was that Quinn took himself off the Straight Talk Express where most of the day-to-day decisions would be made.

The rumor fit the national press's South Carolina stereotype perfectly, and so in the frenzy of the campaign it could not be adequately refuted. During the final days of the race, a number of national reporters and columnists and talking heads continued circulating the purported Quinn dossier without checking its accuracy. Only Tim Russert of *Meet the Press* bothered to check it out. But it was too late.

Neutralizing Quinn was just the beginning.

Just as the McCain campaign had recruited Richard Quinn to manage South Carolina, the Bush campaign had hired a number of operatives whose expertise was various constituencies in the state. In politics at all levels it's essential to find experienced local people and place trust in them. No one person can keep track of all the political nuances. So, like Indian fighters, good managers hire guides along the way.

The Bush 2000 campaign was managed by Karl Rove, the Texas-based political consultant who orchestrated Bush's successful campaigns for governor of Texas in 1994 and 1998. Rove is well known for, among other things, managing his campaigns down to their last detail. As Rove looked at the McCain-Bush match-up numbers in South Carolina, it was apparent that the race among traditional Republican voters was close and that its outcome would hinge upon getting nontraditional Republican primary voters to the polls. The antiestablishment McCain would draw independents and crossover Democrats like Elayne Scott from the left. Rove knew Bush should best look on the right for his new voters. That meant attracting voters from conservative religious groups, including the Christian Coalition, most of whom live and go to church in the upcountry west of Columbia.

To accomplish this, Bush and Rove turned to Pat Robertson, the one-time presidential candidate and televangelist, and to Ralph Reed, the former executive director of the Christian Coalition. Reed, a native Georgian, had left the Christian Coalition in 1997 to start up Century Strategy, an Atlanta-based public relations firm whose mission is to get faith-based candidates elected. Robertson and Reed's job was to energize the approximately 250,000 conservative Christian voters who often stay home on primary day, but who are a formidable political force when they are activated in general elections, and get them into the voting booths casting their votes for Bush. Money was no object. At that stage of the campaign, Bush, who did not favor campaign reform, had more money in the bank than McCain, Gore, and Bradley combined. Finding the targets was relatively easy too. Reed, through his Christian Coalition work, had many of the lists of the church-members that the campaign needed, and with the help of Robertson he could easily get the rest. These names and addresses needed only to be cross-checked against voter lists to isolate the approximately quarter-million targets.

What would Reed and Robertson tell these voters? Whatever would make them not vote for John McCain. Their job was to demonize McCain to these 250,000 voters while making sure the fingerprints of the job didn't get tracked before primary day and that there was deniability for the candidate. Here was the classic negative campaign, executed by surrogates hired by other surrogates, the most sophisticated and ruthless one I'm aware of, and the one for the highest stakes of all. That it shattered Ronald Reagan's admonition to Republicans to avoid attacking one another in primaries was of little matter. Winning was all.

Reed in particular performed his task so brilliantly that his success in the upcountry churches made him, and Century Strategy, a darling of the George W. Bush White House, so much so that one of Bush's first 2004 reelection campaign appointments was to name Reed his southeastern campaign director. Here's some of how the job on John McCain was done.

After returning stateside, following his seven years as a POW, McCain was a sales representative for the Budweiser distributorship in Phoenix. This was the distributorship that was owned by Cindy McCain's family.

The Christian groups in the Carolina upcountry, many of which are Baptist based, often advocate temperance. The surrogates made sure the Christian talk radio jocks knew that McCain made his livelihood trying to interest kids in the Phoenix area in the joys of swilling a few Buds.

But that was just the beginning of what the talk show hosts were fed. The surrogates also conveyed that McCain was psychologically unbalanced from being in Viet Cong prison camps for seven years. And while they were rolling on the crazy stuff, they tied in Cindy McCain, whom the McCain Campaign had disclosed was once treated for depression, saying she was a drug addict who had once been caught stealing drugs from a charity. McCain campaign workers also found workers, who would not say for whom they worked, placing a flyer under church-members' windshield wipers that alleged the same thing: that the senator was crazy after seven years in the cage, and that living with him had turned his wife into a junkie.

Long before they decided John should seek the presidency, John and Cindy McCain adopted a daughter, Bridget, of Bangladeshi descent out of an orphanage run by Mother Teresa. Bridget had had some very serious medical problems, and on a visit to Bangladesh Cindy McCain became convinced the girl would need American medical care to save her life, care Cindy McCain offered to pay for and supervise. By the time the stateside care had been administered, the McCains had fallen in love with Bridget, and so they arranged with the orphanage to make the adoption. They are devoted to the child.

The forces whose job it was to demonize McCain had a field day with Bridget. The fourteen-year-old girl was morphed immediately into McCain's illegitimate black child. The story that McCain had an illegitimate black child was then fed so relentlessly to the local press that, according to the senator, at one point in the final days of the campaign, a TV reporter was so sure it was true that with his camera rolling he asked McCain point-blank whether he had an illegitimate black child.

The senator denied the charge, and in his frustration said, "Who is this child? Do you have any information on this child? Do you have some kind of proof that there is such a child?"

To these questions the reporter replied, "It's not my job to prove there is such a child, it's your job to prove there's not."

Keeping track of which supposed illegitimate child was being asked about must have been difficult at times for the senator, because the rumor the surrogates started in upcountry veterans' circles was that McCain had gotten special treatment in the Viet Cong prison camp because he had fathered a Vietnamese child. Before McCain's victory in New Hampshire, no one in South Carolina had heard any of these stories about McCain, but by primary day everyone had heard more than a few of them, so there can be no doubt whatsoever that the demonization was professionally orchestrated.

The rumors were just the beginning. Then there were the push polls. As a senator, McCain had voted, along with Strom Thurmond, Fritz Hollings, and a majority of the senate, in favor of permitting stem cell research. One push poll call went like this: "If you knew that Senator McCain had voted in the United States Senate in favor of using the fetuses of aborted babies for scientific experiments, would you vote for him?"

Another, the factual underpinnings of which, no matter how far-fetched, are mysterious, was reported to have gone as follows: "If you come to learn that when he is elected president, Senator McCain will favor the removal of the charitable exemption status from Christian churches, do you think it will change your opinion of Senator McCain?"

Tracking back to the Cindy McCain depression disclosure, another push poll call went like this: "If you knew that Senator McCain's wife, a possible first lady of the United States, was a drug addict, would it influence your vote in the upcoming Republican presidential primary in which he is running against George W. Bush, the governor of Texas?"

Similar allegations were made in prerecorded phone calls and e-mails. One such e-mail featured photographs of a dead fetus and a smiling John McCain.

Then there was the direct mail. A week before the election,

thousands of Christian conservatives were mailed a letter from what appeared to be a Baptist Church in Kentucky that raised questions about McCain's sexuality and condemned "John McCain's Fag Army." This attack followed Bush's refusal to meet with the GOP gay group, the Log Cabin Republicans, giving as his excuse that they had already endorsed McCain, which they had not.

There was more. During the campaign, the issue of flying the Confederate battle flag over the South Carolina Statehouse in Columbia was raging across the state. McCain's and Bush's public positions were identical: it's a local issue, let the South Carolina legislature decide whether or not to pull down the flag. But that didn't stop the Bush campaign from seeking to exploit the issue during the last week of the campaign. In tens of thousands of prerecorded phone messages from the newly organized Keep It Flying Committee, McCain was accused of pandering to black South Carolinians by quietly telling black groups he favored the removal of the flag from the statehouse dome.

While Bush's campaign was portraying Quinn as a racist to the politically correct national press corps, they were telling the conservative groups that McCain was secretly sympathetic to the NAACP and hostile to Southern heritage.

McCain held his cool throughout. When asked by Quinn whether he would be willing to engage in tactics similar to his opponent's, the senator said emphatically not. "If we have to lie to win, I would rather not win," he said. True to his words in my office, McCain never answered the Bush charges with charges of his own. As difficult as it was—and more than once Cindy McCain was privately reduced to tears by the ugliness of it—the only McCain counterattack was made privately, before a Columbia debate when McCain looked at Bush and, shaking his head, said sadly, "George."

To which Bush responded, classically, "It's politics, John."

To which McCain replied, "Everything isn't politics."

Later in the debate, during a commercial break, Bush tried to grip McCain's hand and assert his deniability in the smear campaign, to which, within earshot of the press, McCain said: "Don't give me that shit, and take your hands off me."

The Bush campaign's federal election commission filings indicate about $8 million were spent in South Carolina in about three weeks. All that was actually spent will probably never be known because so much of the job on McCain was done by "independent" groups whose financials were beyond the requirements of the campaign disclosure laws. But whatever was the total cost, the effort pushed George W. Bush around a crucial corner and saved him the many more millions a state-by-state fight to the convention would have cost.

The turnout in the 2000 primary was the largest in South Carolina's history. Exit polls showed that McCain beat Bush by a hair among Republicans who did not identify with the religious right, but that religiously motivated Republicans voted for Bush in such overwhelming numbers that he easily carried the day. Karl Rove and Pat Robertson had known just what they were doing. On February 19 John McCain was creamed in South Carolina by a 53 to 42 margin. Two weeks later he was out of the race.

I had gone into the whole affair looking for a bridge, but I had quickly come to conclude that win or lose, McCain would not be playing a role in Beaufort getting the bridge it needed. If he won, he'd be out of the senate, and if he lost and stayed in the senate, he'd still be representing Arizona. Presidents build very few bridges, and of all the presidents—had McCain been elected president—to his credit he'd have been the last one to use federal dollars to favor an elected official for his early support.

A couple of months later, I took Lindsey Graham up on his offer and scheduled a trip to Washington. By then I knew that Lindsey would be running in 2002 for Senator Strom Thurmond's seat, after the then one-hundred-year-old Thurmond retired. I arranged to meet with Lindsey and other members of the South Carolina delegation one afternoon in Washington and, now taking the traditional approach, there we hatched a plan to get the seed money for the bridge.

16. Getting Results

IN early 2000, Eric Holowacz, the executive director of the Arts Council of Beaufort County, came to me with an idea. A staff member of his had just come back from Chicago. She had seen the "cows" exhibit—Chicago's public art office had gotten about 400 life-size fiberglass cows, commissioned local artists to paint them, and then displayed them in prominent locations throughout the city. People loved the cows and came from all over to see them. People who would never step into an art museum or art gallery were talking about the images on their favorite cow and what the images meant to them.

When it was time to take down the cows the public art office arranged an auction, and some of the cows brought more than $50,000 at auction, a not insignificant ancillary benefit of the exhibition. The new owners took their cows and displayed them in front of their businesses or in their backyards, where they sat like home run hitters in the off-season.

Meanwhile, communities from around the world were writing to Chicago's Cultural Affairs Office asking to be sent a few cows. The Public Art Office then decided to bring a few of the cows back together, on loan, for a new exhibition.

Eric had written a letter to Chicago's cultural affairs commissioner, Lois Weisberg. It was his view that it would enhance our chances if I wrote to her too, and I said I would. It was a long shot, to be sure, but how hard is it to write a letter?

The next spring and summer of 2000, thirty-six cows from Chicago—wait, it was actually thirty-seven—visited Beaufort. It was a great big deal and everyone in Beaufort loved it, especially the children, and we were in the newspapers from coast to coast.

The story of the thirty-seventh cow goes like this.

Chicago's public art office rounded up thirty-six of their cows from their new owners and arranged for them to be driven (by semitrailer truck) down to Beaufort. On the day the thirty-six cows arrived from Chicago, all the news photographers wanted to take pictures of the cows being unloaded from the back of the eighteen-wheeler. The cows are fiberglass and don't weigh very much—perhaps sixty pounds—so Eric and I obliged the photographers by unloading one of the cows ourselves, with three staffers from Chicago's public art office playing wranglers. As I noted earlier, there are very few photos that are too corny or inappropriate to participate in.

Afterward we were standing around talking to the reporters, and one of the wranglers, Mike Lash, mentioned that there's another cow in Kansas City that they almost rounded up for Beaufort, but that they couldn't get it from Missouri to South Carolina. This one was the Uncle Sam Cow, dressed like Uncle Sam with the top hat and tails, and with a little goatee, it had been a favorite in Chicago. The American Dairy Farmers Association bought it at the auction for many thousands of dollars. "It's still in its crate," he added. "All it needs is a way to get here."

As it happens, I had recently been out to the Recruit Depot at Parris Island to review a graduation. Brigadier General Steve Cheney was then pretty new on his tour at Parris Island and I had just met him, a sandy-haired young guy from California who seemed less rigid than many of his predecessors. So right there, surrounded by these fiberglass cows, I pulled out my cell phone and called him up.

He came right on the line. "How's my favorite general?" I said.

"Great," he answered, as he always did. "How's my favorite mayor?"

"Great," I said. "Look, I've got a PR opportunity for you," and I explained what I had in mind. "I'll bet you could use it in your recruiting ads somehow."

"Great! That's great!" he said in can-do Marine Corps fashion. "We'll throw it on a damn transport."

A couple of days later I heard that the Uncle Sam Cow had arrived at Parris Island.

Some weeks after that, Chicago Mayor Rich Daley and his wife came to Beaufort with Lois Weisberg and a couple of other Chicagoans to check up on their cows. I had them all over for dinner, and it was very nice, so nice that after a little while I found myself wondering, How could a puppy dog like this guy run that great big tough city? I knew his father had been a tough guy. And his brother had just taken over Al Gore's presidential campaign, not a job for the weak of heart.

After dinner we pulled our chairs together, so it was just the two of us, and he asked me to tell him about the challenges I faced. I spoke for a moment about the resistance the city faces from the county as we seek to grow our boundaries.

He said: "It's just politics. You're going to win. Don't hear a word they say."

Then I explained (as I am sure hundreds of mayors across America explain similarly) that traffic is getting worse every month and the state department of transportation is crying poverty and telling us to solve our own transportation problems. Then I came to the point: "I need a bridge. And that's really just the beginning. I need a loop around Beaufort because the city's streets are becoming clogged with people who are just driving through."

Daley said, and I tell this story because it is the way I feel and the way hundreds of other mayors feel: "You know, going to Congress is a terrible job. There's only two things the people there can do. They can get you money and they can cost you money. Who's your congressman?"

I said, "Floyd Spence."

He said, "Well, he's been there a while. He probably knows what to do. Go to Washington and tell Spence you need a new highway. Tell him to stick it in the next transportation appropriations bill."

The matter became somewhat more complicated than that because the new bridge was to be outside the city's limits, and therefore the venture would necessarily be a cooperative one with the county, and the county had other needs elsewhere it considered more pressing. It took me a year to get their transportation consultant to plot our highway on a map. They all acted like the problems were down in Hilton Head and Bluffton, twenty-five miles away. Without a plan there could be no budget, and without some idea what a new highway's going to cost, it's tough to go to Washington and ask for money.

But an opportunity came along to put some pressure on the county council. Because Beaufort County is the fastest-growing county in South Carolina, the county council very correctly decided that the newcomers should bear more of the costs associated with growth and that the way to assign those costs was to impose impact fees. One proposed fee was a transportation impact fee that would be collected from all new construction. Because the cities issue the building permits for projects within the cities, the county needed the cities to agree to collect the county's transportation impact fees too, and then the plan was we'd all throw the money into the common pot to help meet our transportation needs.

I said: "Well, if we're going to collect the money, you're going to have to tell us how the money's going to be spent. Okay, we can agree on the bridge and bypass, but can we agree on where it's going to go and how much it will cost?"

Barry Connor, then the county councilman from Bluffton, the fastest-growing town in South Carolina, which accordingly has tremendous transportation needs, was in the lead for the county on this issue, replied: "You've got to pass this fee. Every day you don't, you're losing money."

I said: "Barry, before we impose the fee we have to know where the highway will go, how much it will cost, some idea where we're going to get the rest of the money, and when we can expect that construction will begin."

He was sputtering mad. If we didn't pass the fee, he thought his district couldn't get their money. But then someone at the county came up with a reasonable compromise: they cut the impact fee program in half geographically, and backed off the fee for our side of the county pending answers to the four questions I'd posed. Then they hurried up the planning which is what I wanted them to do.

When the congress went back into session, at Lindsey Graham's invitation I went to see my delegation, and I did exactly as Daley suggested. I requested an earmark in the next highway appropriations bill. I was promised an earmark in the TEA-21 reauthorization bill, even though it wouldn't be collected for three years, which will be after this book goes to press. So we'll see.

It took another year to get the answers to the four questions. But as this book goes to press, we are putting the impact fee back on with the new bridge and bypass identified as a recipient project. It appears now, therefore, that we have two funding sources coming on line and we can begin planning the corridor. That took four years of constant vigilance.

17. The Direct Threat

WHILE Columbus was discovering the Americas, a Florentine statesman was writing what is still considered to be the political hardball manifesto. The forms of government have changed in the past five hundred years: feudalism has waned, so too have monarchies, democracy has gained in favor, fascism and communism have each come and essentially gone. But men and their greed for treasure and power have changed not one iota since Niccolò Machiavelli wrote *The Prince*.

Machiavelli, one of Western civilization's great political thinkers, devotes a chapter to whether one rules more effectively by being loved or by being feared. In that chapter, the great strategist offers several reasons why it is better to be feared than loved. To me his most compelling argument is "men are less careful how they offend him who makes himself loved than him who makes himself feared." Machiavelli adds another thought: "Nevertheless a Prince should inspire fear in such a fashion that if he do not win love he may escape hate. For a man may very well be feared and not hated, and this will be the case so long as he does not meddle with the property or with the women of his citizens."

Most elected officials would prefer to be loved than feared. Yet the good ones know there must be an element of fear, or respect, if you prefer. It's likewise so that the more divided and squabbling is one's constituency the more fear must be employed to stay on top. The most desirable situation is, of course, that you, as a public official, will never suffer offense because you are both universally loved and universally feared. But that is unrealistic in the context of the greed and the egos that you will find are the coin of the realm in government.

This is where the political threat comes in. You will likely receive such threats and you may find it necessary from time to time to issue one. There are several forms. The first and the most obvious is the direct threat.

The Brooklyn neighborhood, Crown Heights, is home to several different groups of Hassidic Jews, each with thousands of congregants living in close proximity to their schools and synagogues. In 1981, which was an election year, a squabble arose between Koch and the city councilman from Crown Heights, one Noach Dear, who was Orthodox. Because Koch was Jewish, although not Orthodox, the Jewish residents of Crown Heights were a part of Koch's political base, a base that he necessarily guarded closely. Whatever was the cause of the squabble, it was esoteric to anyone who was not schooled in the intricacies of Hassidic Crown Heights. But it was a big deal to Dear, who took to saying unkind and unflattering things about Koch at public meetings in Crown Heights and at city hall.

Noting this, Koch called Dear into his office and said essentially this: "You and I can disagree. We should try not to, but if we must, that's okay. What's not okay is your engaging in *ad hominem* attacks vis-à-vis me. Not okay. If you do that—and you have done that—then what I must do is to find a candidate to run against you. I have begun doing that this week. My candidate may be a slouch. I don't know who I'll get yet, but I'll take the best that I can find. Even if he is a slouch, I don't care. I will raise money for that slouch and I will prop him up against the walls in your district and I will stand next to him and tell people he is the better alternative. I and my slouch may not be able to beat you, Noach, but we will cost you time and we will cost you money and we will cost you aggravation."

In the end Koch did not find a candidate. He didn't have to, because the personal attacks ceased.

Nine out of ten of these political threat situations occur around election time. That is because it is in the months prior to an election that public officials are most vulnerable. Even a good Republican running unopposed in a gerrymandered Republican district feels some transitory vulnerability in the several months right before the election.

There are regional and cultural differences in how to make a threat. In the more genteel South, for example, Koch would have called upon an intermediary, someone both he and Dear trusted, to deliver the threat. The intermediary permits a Noach Dear some more "wiggle room," but the message is far clearer (and more primal) when one shows one's own teeth. There are a thousand examples of intermediaries getting their instructions wrong and thus making things worse.

The direct approach is in my view preferable to intercession by an intermediary, but both methods leave fingerprints. In town politics (where everyone sees everyone on Main Street every month and so there is necessarily more gentility), it is far better to get your threat conveyed accurately and without fingerprints. But how?

18. The Indirect Threat

IN Beaufort there are two or three families whose members have been closely involved in the civic life of the city for several generations. The Harveys are one of these. Another is the Keyserlings. Both families are longtime Democrats.

Leon Keyserling of Beaufort, an economist, was a professor at Columbia University and then chairman of President Truman's council of economic advisers. Leon Keyserling's brother, Herbert Keyserling, who died in 2000, was a beloved country doctor in Beaufort. Dr. Herbert Keyserling's wife, Harriet, grew up in New York. Harriet and Herbert were married during World War II, and after the war they settled down in Herbert's hometown, Beaufort, to raise a family. Once their children were grown, Harriet got involved in local politics.

It was the time of women's liberation and Harriet was in Beaufort's vanguard. She was the first woman to run for the Beaufort County Council, and she was elected. After only two years there, she ran for the South Carolina House of Representatives and was elected. There she served the people of Beaufort with distinction for sixteen years before yielding her seat to her son, Billy, in 1992. In her years commuting to and from Columbia, Harriet was a model of conscience and rectitude. She was a tireless and effective advocate for better education, a healthier environment, and cleaner government. In ways that thrilled her supporters she took the trouble to try to educate the Good Ole

Boys at the statehouse in the areas of the arts and women's issues. It was a thing to see. And, while tiny in stature, Harriet was a giant force on all issues big and small back home in the district.

Billy, who is my age, inherited many of his mother's best qualities. He is, for example, very smart about sizing up political situations and seeing opportunities. And he can be quite charming, which is helpful in political situations. He is, by virtue of his birth, well connected in South Carolina political circles, and he is well familiar with the ways in which those who are connected may use those connections. In addition, Billy's mother is devoted to him.

For many years Billy was an out-of-town celebrity because he lived in Washington, where he was involved with politics on the large scale, running a human rights organization and managing Fritz Hollings's 1984 presidential bid, for example. When he returned to Beaufort in 1990, it wasn't long before his mother began arranging to hand her House seat over to him.

Beaufort being a small town and Billy and I having had similar work backgrounds, for several years just after Billy moved back to town we tried to be friends. But there seemed to be something in the way. A few years later, during my first years on the city council and while Billy was still in the House, we worked together some.

One of the things good local officials do is keep up with the sources of funding coming available from the state and federal governments and then arrange to get in on the new fad. There are a hundred ways to twist around the funding criteria of new federal and state grant programs so that they are made to describe legitimate things that are needed in your community.

In 1994, greenways were a new phenomenon in South Carolina when I proposed that Beaufort get into the greenway game.

Ken Driggers at the Palmetto Conservation Foundation was responsible for a model project pot of greenway money. The higher-ups at the South Carolina Parks, Recreation, and Tourism agency (PRT) had told him that he should review the applications and work with the winner to make sure the model project came out all right. Ken called me up and said, "Beaufort ought to apply." And we did. There were very few applicants.

After a short stint in the public relations/political consulting area in Beaufort, Billy Keyserling had gone into real estate. By 1994 that was his day job. His night job was representing both Beaufort and Port Royal in the South Carolina House. As a part of his real estate activities, Billy was planning what became a very successful neotraditional in-fill housing development in Port Royal, the town next door to Beaufort.

Up in Columbia, Billy heard about PRT's greenway money. So he called the town manager in Port Royal and told him to put in an application, which Port Royal did. Billy probably didn't know that my friend Ken Driggers was going to be the judge. As the time neared for PRT to announce who would receive the $312,000 model project grant, Billy turned up the pressure on PRT, importuning them to choose Port Royal. Driggers reviewed the applications, and he chose Beaufort. Upon hearing the news, Billy reportedly hit the roof and called PRT demanding that they reconsider. Remember, he's in the House representing both towns.

The higher-ups at PRT called Driggers and said: "Rep. Keyserling's on the warpath, you've gotten us into trouble with him, you have to give the money to Port Royal." Ken, who's very savvy, called me and we talked about it. We decided that Ken should call Billy and explain to him that I knew that he was trying to take away Beaufort's money, and that I was pretty steamed up about it, and that I probably wouldn't be able to keep quiet about it for very long. The next day Ken called me back and said he'd talked to Billy and it had all been a misunderstanding and that Beaufort, which Billy had noted to Driggers was in Billy's district too, would get the money uncontested.

Soon thereafter Billy stepped down from his legislative duties to devote full time to his real estate activities. The two-city-block development in Port Royal, which is known locally as "Billyville," was under way and Billy was looking around for other opportunities.

Right after Billy had moved back to Beaufort, he had run David Taub's successful campaign for mayor of Beaufort. It had been a good campaign, especially since David (who turned out to be a good mayor) was just a fair-weather campaigner. David and Billy became good friends in that campaign, and when David announced in 1997 that he wouldn't be running for reelection, he began hinting that his logical successor should be Billy.

By then I had been the mayor pro tem for several years, so as Billy and David surveyed the political landscape, I'm sure my name came up on their screens. First David was detailed to tell me how great Billy was and how great the two of us would be working together. And of course if I stood aside by declining to seek the mayorality, Mayor Billy would support my continuing as mayor pro tem. That went on for several months.

I always listened in studied silence. Sometimes, just to throw some confusion into the picture, I'd say things that implied I didn't want the mayor's job. But as the pregnant pauses got longer, I said less and less. It was a long time until the election and I didn't want David hindering my efforts to build my record.

About a year before the election, I ran into Billy at a Hollings fundraiser at Brantley Harvey's house. He came over to talk and he obviously had something on his mind. He said, "I think I'm going to run for mayor. What are you going to do?" Words to that effect. I knew what I was going to do, but I still didn't want David Taub, who was giving me carte blanche and with whom I was working well, to freeze up on me.

So I just answered the first part. I said, "I think you should run." The fact is, I always say that to everyone. If they ask you, they've probably already made up their minds. So all that can happen is you make them mad at you if you tell them not to run. This is America. Everyone should run! Probably he was hoping I'd say something like "I'll support you for mayor if you'll support me for mayor pro tem and put me in charge of the parks and the police, let's work together," a quid pro quo in which he goes first and gets a lot and doesn't have to give much. Who wouldn't? But I was under no obligation to tell him whether I would run, so I just disengaged from him as gracefully as I could.

As the filing date for the election approached, various other people (including the ever-persistent David Taub) tried to wheedle out of me what I was going to do. But I kept my answers vague. I suspected that the news that I was going to run wouldn't keep anyone else from running. But why not lure as many as possible into the field, and try to win in a three- or four-way contest? The rules were that there would be no runoff, so I could theoretically win a four-way race with 26 percent of the vote. I figured I could ring that many doorbells.

A month before the conclusion of the filing period, Billy called me. I was up in Camden, South Carolina, taking Reed Buckley's public speaking course. "I'm running," he said. "I just wanted you to hear it from me."

My sense was he wanted me to say something like "You'll be

terrific" or "It'll be great working together." I just said: "Thanks for letting me know. I appreciate that."

Because of low voter turnout in previous mid-May city elections, David Taub had suggested a better calendar: that mayor and two councilmembers should run when the presidents run, and the other two council-members should run with the off-year congressional candidates. Council agreed with his suggestion and, accordingly, the term that we would be running for was only seventeen months. But since it was for an empty seat there was expected to be a lot of interest.

The first person officially into the race was my fellow councilmember Donnie Beer, who had the signatures on her petitions and had them handed in three weeks before the deadline. Next in was a surprise, former mayor Henry Chambers. There was a lull, and then with great fanfare in came Billy.

With four days to go before the filing deadline, I began collecting my signatures.

I probably started out dead last, which actually isn't a bad place to start. The reporters are kinder to you, and a little kindness from the press early on in an election can go a long way. Because the former mayor, Henry Chambers, had been in real estate for so long, and because the people of Beaufort were beginning to get nervous about too much development, I thought I might be able to take him.

Mrs. Beer's position on taxes had been so often stated by her and was so odd (she believes the tax rate should be increased a little bit each year, whether the government needs the money or not) that I figured I could rely on the differences between her view and mine—following Machiavelli's admonition to keep the government's hands off the people's property, I say government should raise taxes only as a last resort.

But Billy might have been harder to beat. His way of wrapping himself in his mother's ethical, environmental, and arts mantle brought to him the very people who would normally be put off by a real estate developer. In addition, all his real estate developments were in Port Royal, so he could honestly say—and his mother was saying it—that he didn't have any financial interests in Beaufort real estate development. Moreover, it hadn't been so long since he had been in the South Carolina House, so he still had access to the standing organization he had inherited from his very popular and highly organized mother. I felt certain he could also raise the money he would need, because if nothing else, his mother would help him with that too.

Within a couple of days of my arrival in the race, an interesting thing began to happen. People who had been observing Billy's activities in Port Royal began to show up at my doorstep. Reporters get used to situations like these, but it had been a while since I'd been a reporter, so it was a little startling. One person called up and wouldn't give his name. I said, "Okay, well, what can I do for you?"

He said, "I have some information I think you'll find interesting."

I said, "Oh? Like what?"

He said, "I can't tell you over the phone. It has to do with your campaign."

"Well, do you want to send it to me?"

"No," he said. "I have to explain it to you."

"Okay, well do you want to come by my office?"

"No, I don't want anyone to see me coming into your office."

"Okay, shall I come over?"

"No. I don't want anyone to see you at my house."

"Okay, so what's your suggestion?"

"Let's meet in the Wal-Mart parking lot in fifteen minutes."

"Okay, fifteen minutes. How will I know you?"

"You won't need to," he said. "I know you. Just pull into the parking lot and wait for me. And don't bring anybody with you."

Fifteen minutes later I pulled into the parking lot, and Deep Throat here emerged with a package of deeds and Port Royal town planning studies and newspaper stories that he said showed what amounted to a form of insider trading on Billy's part. The allegation was to the effect that Billy had known in advance where the interstate and its interchanges were going to be sited, then before the news was made public, he optioned the farms where the interchanges would go. I just put the stuff aside.

Not every call I got was so mysterious, but within a couple of weeks various people had dropped off quite a collection of materials alleging Billy's supposed misdeeds in Port Royal. The question then became what to do with it. I had been in campaigns where damaging materials came in at the last desperate moment and if there had only been more time they might have been used to good effect. Legitimately, in the last week or ten days of a campaign newspaper editors get very cautious about using materials that could be damaging to one or another candidacy. So I knew one thing not to do was to wait for later. Neither did I say anything about what I had to anyone, nor even hint I had something.

Finally it hit me. There is a lawyer who practices in the Beaufort area (friendly with both Billy and me) who loves to yak about politics. I called him up and said: "People have been bringing me this stuff and saying terrible things about Billy. I don't know what's true or not. You're a savvy guy. You read the papers and you know more about what goes on in Port Royal than I do. What do you say you look over this stuff and see if there's anything there?"

He said, "Sure," and I could tell he was licking his chops. After a few days, he returned the materials to me. I never looked at the stuff myself. My guess is there was nothing there that would have been of interest to the local newspapers, much less the solicitor. Billy's an honest man. He's just not an outsider. His business interests are tied to the establishment, which is after all just the kind of elected official who was envisioned by Alexander Hamilton.

But the dossier rumor had begun to spread, and the power of rumors in politics should never be discounted. Two weeks later, in his opening statement at the first mayoral candidates debate, Billy pulled out of the race, explaining that he wouldn't have enough time to attend to his business obligations and be mayor too.

Billy's abrupt exit gave rise to a new rumor that he and Henry Chambers had met and decided that rather than run against one another they should share the mayoralty—that Billy would get out now and let Henry be mayor for seventeen months and "kick some ass" (meaning "bring back some Chambers loyalists who had left"), and then Henry would "turn it over" to Billy. Since I hadn't had to give up my council seat to run, I felt sure another one of the asses Henry had in mind for kicking was mine. But I loved the rumor, coming especially as it did right at the beginning of the race, and so did my supporters, because it made Henry sound so much like a Good Ole Boy who was accustomed to manipulating the system.

Other than that, however, Billy withdrew with great grace and little rancor. The same did not hold true for his mother, however, who couldn't bring herself to do anything but glare at me for at least a year.

Rumors can be effective, but they are not the only tool in the toolbox. There are other, stronger ways to threaten your opponents without leaving fingerprints.

That frosty twelve months brought us to the eve of when candidates wishing to challenge me would begin to make their moves in advance of the November 2000 election. Henry had obviously been exhausted, and the margin over Donnie had been such that it was clear she shouldn't try again so soon. In that short time, there had been no new players into the game. So that left Billy.

And Billy was being mysterious. He went to a spa and lost, it was said, twenty-five pounds. He gave my newly estranged wife a job decorating one of his buildings. He started showing up at public meetings where, so far as anyone knew, he had no private interest. And he was running around asking people how they thought I'd been doing as mayor.

The only issue in the city that had caused any controversy during my first year as mayor had been the city's efforts to extend its boundaries along commercial corridors just outside the city's limits as a way of enhancing the city's revenues. Some people who lived just outside the city's limits wished that the city wouldn't grow. They were able to enjoy most of the quality-of-life benefits of living in Beaufort without having to pay city taxes. They feared the city's expansion would somehow engulf them, and they would lose their subsidy.

One of these not-so-good neighbors of the city's was Sam Jewell. In 2000 Sam lived just outside the city's limits in a beautiful house that is situated on three lots in a tony subdivision that looks out across the Beaufort River at downtown Beaufort. The place features a swimming pool, a woodworking shop, and a gymnasium. Fancying himself a countryman because he lives on so many lots, Sam kept a couple of sheep for pets penned in his front yard along the riverbank.

Now Sam and I had had an interesting history. Even though he did not live in the city per se, he had been one of my most enthusiastic supporters in 1999. And even though he was a big fan of Harriet Keyserling's, he had waded deeply into the race on my side. He had even, or at least he told me he had even, in the 1999 race sent Billy a check for $50 accompanied by a nasty note telling him he thought that anyone with Billy's real estate interests ought not to be running for mayor. To Billy's credit, I was subsequently told, Billy sent the check back to Sam accompanied by a few words of his own.

A year later, however, and now steamed up about the city's expansion on to Lady's Island where Sam lived, Sam had reportedly called Billy up and sought to recruit him to run against me. Sam was also by then the ringleader of a group of his neighbors that he had organized for the purpose of raising money to pay lawyers to contest the city's growth. As a part of that effort, Sam had a list of e-mail addresses of people who had, presumably, expressed to him their support for his group's efforts.

In another hardball classic, Sun Tzu's *The Art of War* (written in approximately 500 B.C.), there is a chapter on spies that is a real eye-opener. Sun begins by explaining that "what enables the wise sovereign and the good general to strike and conquer, and achieve things beyond the reach of ordinary men, is foreknowledge." He then goes on to describe five kinds of spies: the local, the inward, the converted, the doomed, and the surviving spy. When information on the enemy's intentions and movements is gleaned from competent practitioners in each of those five categories, wrote Sun, and when that information is assembled and analyzed by the sovereign, it becomes "the divine manipulation of the threads that is the sovereign's most precious faculty."

Well, I didn't have five different kinds of spies in Sam's group, but I had a couple and they were enough to keep me apprised of his activities. As it happened, just as Billy Keyserling was acting as if he might run against me in November 2000, Sam Jewell was looking for a city resident who would, in order to get standing before the court, act as a plaintiff in one of Sam's lawsuits against the city.

One morning about ten o'clock, Sam sent out an e-mail to his supporters soliciting ideas for a plaintiff, and by eleven one of my spies had forwarded it to me. It was full of distortions, including some language to the effect that the city had issued permits for six building units to be built on a parcel of property that was down the street from his house, and that this was going to pollute the river and adversely affect his property values or some such foolishness. In fact the city had permitted no more than three units on the parcel and they would all have to get septic tanks approved by the state, and if they didn't build right away they would probably soon enjoy access to a sanitary sewer. Under most circumstances I would have ignored the whole thing. But I was interested to look over the names of the recipients to see who Sam's supporters were. It happened that Billy was one of them.

That got me to thinking that this might be an excellent time to remind Billy how messy running against me might be and to send a rocket into Sam's headquarters in the bargain, thus chilling the enthusiasm of anyone who might be considering lending his name to Sam's lawsuit.

I logged onto Hotmail.com and created a new e-mail address

more or less untraceable to me, then addressed a message to everyone on Sam's list, with a copy to Sam. The message began by asking why Sam felt the need to exaggerate what the city had permitted by way of density; went on to observe that Sam, who says he is a fighter against suburban sprawl, lives on three suburban lots; and concluded by observing that the shit from Sam's sheep that washes untreated into the Beaufort River every day unquestionably pollutes the river more than any six houses anywhere in the county. I sent the e-mail out about three o'clock that afternoon. Sam and his crowd knew I had done it. Good. I wanted them to. But they couldn't prove it, so it couldn't become the subject of discussion with reporters. My nasty little e-mail just sat there and rankled.

To gain standing for his lawsuit, Sam was reduced to relying upon a county employee who, I believe, was under pressure from his supervisor. The complainant was certainly no one who was brought in by the e-mail. Shortly afterward, Billy announced he'd be running for one of the two city council seats that were opening up. Again, it was explained, he was too busy to be mayor.

I ran unopposed for reelection in 2000. Billy won too, and three years into it we have a good working relationship that has served Beaufort well, as for example when we teamed up in 2002 to beat the penny sales tax.

19. Mean It

FEW things diminish an elected official's effectiveness among his colleagues more than becoming known as someone who doesn't deliver what he promises. Therefore, threats should not be made lightly, but when one has been made, self-preservation requires that you make your best efforts to deliver the threatened consequences, should that become necessary.

In early 2002, reacting to complaints about traffic tie-ups on Hilton Head Island's major corridor, U.S. 278, Beaufort County Council Chairman Tom Taylor announced the county would seek to impose a special purpose countywide penny sales tax, the proceeds from which would be used for transportation. Taylor represented one of three Hilton Head districts. The imposition of a temporary sales tax requires a majority vote of the registered voters in Beaufort County. The tax had been used successfully a few years before to fund the widening of the road that connects the southern part of the county to its northern part, SC 170. As the announcement was made, the general feeling around the county was that the penny tax to widen U.S. 278 would be a winner with the voters too.

But there was a consideration with the U.S. 278 proposal that hadn't been present with the SC 170 one. U.S. 278 begins on Hilton Head Island just outside Charles Frazer's famous Sea Pines development, runs west past Bluffton where SC 170 splits off to go to Beaufort, and finally connects with Interstate 95 at Hardeeville. It is the major east-west corridor of southern Beaufort County, but at its closest point it's still fifteen miles from U.S. 278 to the Beaufort city limits. "What's in this for us?" I asked.

Initially, Taylor tried to reuse the winning SC 170 argument, saying Beaufort people work in Hilton Head and they would benefit from the newly widened road. That statement offended all of the Beaufort City Council, who simply didn't accept it, and prompted us to begin talking among ourselves about what we would need in order to support Taylor's proposal.

Billy Keyserling astutely observed that it's much easier to defeat a ballot measure that calls for the voters to tax themselves than it is to get it passed. "When these things pass," he said, "it's because everyone's for it." Council concurred, and we began considering what project or projects we thought should be added to the U.S. 278 improvements in order that our support might be gained.

The historic downtown center of Beaufort began becoming the retail center of the city over two hundred years ago. Like all commercial areas that were built before the automobile, no parking lots were planned, and for all its charm and central location, it's not as easy to park downtown—especially when downtown's busy—as it is at the malls. For years the city's leadership had talked about the need for a municipal parking garage, but no one had ever figured out a way to pay for it.

About that time, Tom Taylor sent a letter to all four mayors in the county asking them to caucus their staffs and their counsels, and suggest to him transportation projects that might be added to U.S. 278. He was beginning to see political reality. The city council formally considered his request and sent Taylor back a letter describing the parking garage, the need for it, and its $6.5 million cost. Our letter wasn't very well received by Taylor and some of the other council-members. I think they thought we should be sending them a road-widening project, but Taylor had asked and we had responded, and we were disinclined to alter our view.

A few weeks later at a county intergovernmental relations committee meeting, which is where the four mayors in the county and the county council get together to talk about matters of common interest, the talk turned to the list of projects. I said, "For us to support it, there's got to be a reason. There's got to be something in there that benefits Beaufort."

Taylor said, "You mean your votes are for sale?"

I said: "Well, I wouldn't characterize it just like that, Tom, but to me it's Politics 101 that people vote for things that are in their interests and they vote against things that aren't, particularly when what they're voting on is taxing themselves."

In public comments over the next few days the mayor pro tem, Donnie Beer, Councilman Billy Keyserling, and I all said we wouldn't be able to support a ballot measure that didn't include the garage.

Taylor didn't formally say yes, nor did he give us a formal no. He went out to play golf, which was his custom. All work and no play was never the Taylor way. As the deadline for finalizing the ballot language approached, Council discussed its options and, at Billy's suggestion, we put together a list of projects that we thought could win a majority of the county council's support. It was substantially different from the one Taylor was promoting, but it included the $28.5 million that had been talked about as the amount needed to widen SC 278 . . . and it included the $6.5 million for the parking garage.

★ ★ ★ ★ ★ ★ ★ ★ ★ ★ ★ ★ ★ ★ ★

20. Leaking

THERE'S a great old building right behind city hall in New York that
in 1979 was called the Tweed Courthouse. In recent years it has
been reused as the chancellor of the board of education's offices
and as a school called City Hall Academy. In 1979 it was a city
office building, and a tomb. You could hear your steps echo
throughout its massive halls. Clerks walked slowly and by themselves through its halls, sometimes carrying large files containing
hundreds of sheets of paper that no one cared about any more.
This was the mausoleum of the living dead of city government.
It's also where my first office was.

Fifty yards away in the Koch City Hall, groups of decision-
makers hurried from office to office. Others stood in clumps in
the narrow back halls before and after meetings. They spoke ex-
citedly. Sometimes they strained four and five at a time, one looking over another's shoulder, to simultaneously read the freshly
drafted words on important sheets of paper. Secretaries' desks
were jammed into anterooms in such ways as to assure that not
another desk could be squeezed in. Phones rang on these desks
incessantly, and aggressive-looking young people could be seen
leaning over the secretaries and barking into two phones at once
while holding a third in their armpit.

One day in 1979, I was walking over from city hall to the
Tweed Courthouse and down one of those huge empty halls to

my office. As I was walking, an old man came up to me. I had never seen him before, but he knew my name. He said to me, "Mr. Rauch, be careful to be decent to the people you see on your way up . . . because you will see the same faces on your way down."

I have never forgotten what that man said to me and I hope I have lived by it. Why do I mention it here? To leak effectively, three elements must be present. You must have good information that has been tightly held. It may come from a lowly secretary, or an anonymous voice on the phone, or from the governor. You must also have a relationship of trust with at least one reporter. And you must have the sense to know when publicizing what you have learned will help you. I cannot help you with the third element except to say that you get better at this by doing it.

As to building the necessary relationships with sources and reporters, there is no better advice than that which the old man gave to me.

Before I was the press secretary for Mayor Koch, I was a special assistant to the mayor for about a year. During that year my job was to acclimate a new deputy mayor, Ken Lipper, then the deputy mayor for finance and economic development, to political life. Ken was a brilliant deal-maker from Salomon Brothers, but his day-to-day political experience was limited. He was also the first deputy mayor in the Koch administration to have oversight of the Office of Management and Budget (OMB), an agency that had been reporting directly to the mayor for five years. My job was first to watch Ken's back around city hall, which was no mean feat since the newly disenfranchised folks at OMB are well known to be the toughest breed of bureaucrat. After that it was centives than Ken had been prepared to offer. The "toxic waste dump" leak shut down Shearson's alternative. Three months later, Shearson announced the company would be availing itself of a raft of city-arranged incentives and building its ten-story, $500 million computer complex in lower Manhattan. We estimated 3,400 jobs, including 2,200 new ones, and $25 million a year in taxes had been at stake. But the real bonus would be next door. There, Shearson announced, in phase two the company would build its headquarters, a forty-story, $300 million building. Interviewed at the time of the announcement of the Manhattan deal, Cohen said of the company's contemplated move to Newport City: "We were very close to signing a deal."

For the sake of definitions, let's look at these words. The "press release" that Shearson issued was a piece of paper that got faxed to many newspapers, and it was played all around as a business brief. The *Times* story was a "leak," so it went to just one paper. The "exclusive" nature of the story was made clear to the reporter by me. The story was a hot one and the *Times* had it alone, so it got the best possible placement.

Now let's turn to the leak itself. You've chosen the paper and the reporter. Now, when you leak, how do you do it so as to protect your anonymity?

First, don't call a reporter you don't know. With a reporter you do know, and with whom you have worked, there is great flexibility. It is also true that some newspapers have more integrity when it comes to "sourcing" than do others. The *Times*, for example, has the strictest policy but they run plenty of "blind," or anonymously sourced, pieces, especially involving government. At other papers it may be possible to further cover your tracks by getting the reporter to describe you as someone you clearly are not. An example of this would be receiving a tip from the mayor and having the news she conveyed attributed to "a Capitol Hill source" in the paper.

Assuming there's trust in the relationship, the basic conversation goes like this:

"Howard, this is Bill. I've got a story for you."

"Yeah, Bill," Howard says. "How are you? What's going on?"

"A lot," I say, "and you're going to want to be the first to write about it. But before I go on, I have to know we're off the record. No fingerprints. My name or where I'm from nowhere near your story."

"Okay," says Howard, "we're off the record."

"Okay. Now you know about that headquarters Shearson announced a couple of days ago they were looking at building in Jersey . . ."

Why all the trouble? The purpose of leaking is to influence decision-making without adversely affecting your own position. If you were to allow the sourcing to be attributed to you or even to city hall, two things would happen. The other people in the deal might not talk to you anymore, and the story, by being attributed to you or your side, would lose credibility.

It's vitally important, then, that the quoting and sourcing discussion be done and specifically agreed to by the reporter *before* you reveal the substance of the story. If you don't get the rules the way you want them, don't reveal the substance.

That leads us to what happens after the story appears. Immediately everyone who was supposed to be keeping the secret that is now in the paper calls everybody else and tries to figure out how the reporter got the story. I learned this part from Bobby Wagner, the son of a great New York mayor and the grandson of a great senator from New York and himself a consummate backroom operator. "Never admit it," Bobby told me. "Even when you're the only one who could have done it, deny it and deny it," he added. Bobby was right. The reporter won't give you up. You have just made him the toast of the town for a day. Only you can give yourself up. Don't do it.

You can use leaks for offensive moves, as was done with Shearson, and you can use leaking defensively. If you know bad news is coming, you can take a lot of the edge off the harmful story by leaking it to the right reporter. That way your reporter gets the story first and, in exchange for the exclusive, shapes the story so that it's less harmful to its source. If you ask, the reporter may even help see to it that the story gets buried deep in the paper where it's less likely to be given importance by the reader. Contrary to expectation, however, page five's better than page fifty-five.

Here's why. After the first-day story appears, the other reporters on the beat will have been made to look bad by missing the story, and they may become angry and vow revenge. When they call, ignore their anger. If they're calling about the story that ran in today's paper, they're going to be reporting on yesterday's news, and their editors are going to put their stories where old news goes, on the back pages. But that is true only if the initial story could be found by the average reader leafing through her morning paper. If the leaked story was buried too deeply, however, the editors at the other papers may conclude that they can wrap a few new facts around it and still play it as their front page news.

Managing bad news is a high political art. This is what keeps the best of the PR consultants in their limos. A well-timed, well-placed leak can start a bad story off on its best foot, or—to use the term that's preferred today—with the best spin.

21. Spinning

SPINNING is taking a negative and turning it into a positive. It is amending a story that's already out there to enhance your own position. If you are adept enough at spinning, as far as the public is concerned, you've never been surprised and you have never made a mistake.

In the summer of 1985, three city hall reporters, one each from the *Times*, the Associated Press, and United Press International, authored a book about Koch. In preparing the book, they interviewed a number of people who had known Ed for many years. Some of these were no longer friendly with Ed, and among that group were Jack Newfield, a reporter for *The Village Voice*, and David Schneiderman, the *Voice*'s editor. In these interviews Newfield recalled Ed referring to California Congressman Ron Dellums as "the Watusi from Berkeley," and Schneiderman recalled Ed saying once in Washington he had looked up to see "this Zulu warrior standing before me," and that it had been Dellums. Dellums is black, and in Congress he was well known for supporting the interests of the Palestinians, thus making him a natural adversary of Koch who stood up for Israel. Both African nation references were included in the reporters' book.

During the difficult budget years of his first mayoral term, Ed had authorized the city's health and hospitals corporation to close down outmoded Sydenham Hospital in Harlem, which was the first hospital in New York where many black doctors had found work, and as such the hospital had become a cultural shrine. At the same time, after the federal government threatened to withdraw its funding from the city's antipoverty programs, his administration restructured the programs to curtail corruption and increase services—meaning, inevitably, that some employees with political connections, many of whom were African American, lost their jobs.

As a result of these two policy directives, Ed was harshly criticized by some influential black leaders: Congressman Charlie Rangel, Reverend Calvin Butts, and Reverend Al Sharpton come to mind as three who unashamedly played the race card. From then on Ed had increasingly strained relations with the black leadership, and those strains undoubtedly contributed to his loss in the 1989 Democratic primary to David Dinkins, a Harlem clubhouse politician.

I never thought Ed was a racist, and I still don't. The problem was, characteristically, he never shied away from discussing race as forthrightly as he discussed politics, food, art, or what was playing at the movies. He was philosophically opposed to affirmative action, and he refused to pander by engaging in public bloodlettings over the wrongs of the past, whether against blacks, Palestinians, Jews, the American Indian Sioux Nation, the Bahai, or the Inca. His candor inevitably led to demagogues characterizing him as a racist.

In a leak, but not from me, several weeks before the book's publication date, George Artz of the *New York Post* had gotten the galleys of the other three city hall reporters' book, and he came to see me when he got in to work and showed me the Dellums passage. I was the press secretary at the time. "I'm going to use this for a column item and I'm going to need a comment from

the mayor about this," he added, showing me the Dellums references. The *Post*, in a grandstand play, would be the first newspaper to print the revelations made in the new Koch book. If I had
leaked it myself, George's column, "Around City Hall," is just
where I'd have placed the story. It was well read, mostly by insid-
ers, but placed well into the paper. I said, "Give me until lunch,"
which still gave George plenty of time to write his story.

In the little time I had available, I dispatched my best re-
searcher, Assistant Press Secretary Leland Jones, to the nearby
Pace University library where the mayor's office had reading and
research privileges. His instructions were to find and copy all references to anything good about Watusi royalty and Zulu warriors.
Forty-five minutes or so later Jones was back with the materials.
I combed through them to find what I believed were the references that best portrayed our case. Then I called George.

We met in the crowded main hall of city hall just outside the
press office. I said, "Okay, what's your question?"

He said, "Well, in the book the mayor makes these references
to Congressman Dellums looking like a Watusi prince and a Zulu
warrior. Isn't that racial stereotyping? Isn't that pejorative? Isn't
that racist?"

I said: "Absolutely not. Anyone with any background in
African history would immediately know that these are great
compliments. The Zulu nation was comprised of the most courageous of warriors. They beat the Boers, after all. And the Watusi
are known to be the noblest in features and courage of the African nations. George, you need to bone up on your African
history." And then I handed him Jones's research.

He looked at me as if I had lost my mind. But however out-
landish they seemed to be, George carried my comments in his
column the next day.

That morning I ran into Bronx County Democratic Leader Stanley Friedman in the hall. A very, very smart guy with a wonderfully engaging manner, a former deputy mayor under Abe Beame, Stanley was Roy Cohn's law partner at the time. If there was ever a political fixer who enjoyed the role, it was Stanley. He knew everybody, who was up and who was down, and why, and how it could be of use to him.

Stanley was also a master of that conspiratorial Bronx way of signaling with the shoulders that he wanted to talk to you privately, to share a secret with you. So Stanley called me over, assumed the conspirator's stance and said, grinning through his goatee: "That was the goddamnedest story I ever read. About those Watusi princes and whatever the hell they were. If my ass ever really gets in a crack, I'm calling you to get me out."

The Dellums references were soon forgotten, as was the reporters' book. And, alas, a few weeks later Stanley was fingered by U.S. Attorney Rudolph Guiliani as a conspirator in a city contract bid-rigging scheme that engulfed city hall in scandal. But that is a story for a later chapter.

Sometimes spinning is jujitsu, as it was with the reporters' book, and sometimes it's sleight of hand, as was the case with the following watercress incident.

About a month before the 1985 primary against Carol Bellamy, Ed Koch was well ahead. And we were feeling pretty good about things. As was Ed's custom, once or twice a week he would gather up Dan Wolf and a couple of staffers and we'd slip out for a quick lunch at one of those little family-run restaurants on Mott Street in Chinatown. Ed generally ordered for everyone, and all the various plates heaped with Chinese delicacies were placed on a lazy susan and shared by the group. When the meal was concluded Ed got the check, did the arithmetic, and we'd all go Dutch. Maybe it would be $12 apiece.

Well on this occasion, just after the first plates had been put on the lazy susan and the group had begun eating, Ed suddenly stood up and held his hands to his throat in the universal sign of choking. Sitting next to Ed was David Margolis, the CEO of Colt Industries at the time and a very close friend of Ed's. David's wife, Bobbie, was the city's liaison to the UN and to the international community generally. Reacting very swiftly, David, who is at least eight inches shorter than Ed and seventy-five pounds lighter, jumped up, grabbed Ed around the chest with both arms, put his fist into Ed's solar plexus, and gave him a quick, firm upward hug. Whatever had been lodged in Ed's throat was sprung free by David's skillful administering of the Heimlich maneuver. Ed took a long, rather noisy breath, gave a quick smile and wave indicating he was okay to a few of the other—by then shocked—diners in the restaurant, and then sat back down and resumed his lunch where he had left off.

But of course it wasn't as simple as that. Before he got back to city hall the phones in the press office started ringing: "We understand the mayor nearly choked to death at lunch. That he was only saved by the Heimlich maneuver! We want to talk to him about it. How is he? We want to see him! When will he be available?"

Well, there was a problem. The culprit was a piece of pork, and the waiter, who would inevitably soon be interviewed by the reporters, may have known what was on Ed's plate. A month before the primary Ed didn't need it known in the Orthodox Jewish community that he was in the habit of going over to Chinatown to have pork for lunch. But, characteristically, he certainly wasn't going to lie either, at least not by commission.

The finest minds on the City Hall staff were gathered in Ed's office. The question was asked: "Well, besides pork, what else was in the dish?"

"I don't know what you call most of that stuff," Ed replied, "but there was watercress in there too."

That was it. The story was he choked on some watercress. But that wasn't all of it. It had quite clearly been the Heimlich maneuver that had saved him, and Ed said, "It needs to be dramatized."

At that stage the city's health commissioner was summoned to city hall. Ed told him the story, including the watercress and the Heimlich maneuver. Of course the commissioner was familiar with the Heimlich maneuver and he began citing the shocking and little known statistics on the many, many people who die from choking each year. Year in and year out, choking is one of the top five non-illness-related causes of death, he said. And most people have never heard of the Heimlich maneuver. Many fewer have had actual practice performing it. Lives could be saved. Hundreds of lives could be saved! He got right into it.

About four o'clock that afternoon we called a press conference. The Blue Room was packed. It was an international story: "Mayor of New York saved from choking to death in Chinatown restaurant."

Through the course of the half-hour session, every time a reporter asked what Ed had choked on, he would mutter something about watercress and then extol the virtues of his friend David Margolis and those of Dr. Heimlich and his maneuver. The two had teamed up to save Ed's life. The matter was of such importance that forthwith the health department was going to have posters made up illustrating how the Heimlich maneuver is performed and require every restaurant to display the poster.

During the afternoon that day a *New York Post* reporter went to Chinatown and found the waiter who had brought the food to the table. The next day the waiter was quoted as saying, as I recall it, "The mayor talk, talk, talk and eat. He eat too much while talking . . ." Not a word about pork.

Ed beat Carol Bellamy handily the next month, and he ran very strongly (as he always did) in the Orthodox Jewish community.

And that is how those blue and orange posters got into all the restaurants in New York.

22. Creating Cover

CREATING political cover is the practice of finding someone else somewhere else who can be made primarily responsible for a decision that might be harmful or painful for some one or group you wish not to alienate. The skilled politician recognizes well in advance a situation that may adversely affect some group down the line. If such an adverse outcome is likely because one group can only be placated at the expense of another, then the politician may seek to find someone to blame for the controversial outcome—someone to hide behind.

The city attorney is sometimes useful in this regard, generally in situations that involve the interpretation of a law. An unpopular decision can often be explained by saying, essentially, that the government has to do it this way or we'll be sued and we'll lose and then we'll have to pay precious tax dollars to cover the damages.

But when it comes to changing local laws and policies, the city attorney offers only limited cover. Here a more comprehensive insulation mechanism is needed—"the blue ribbon panel." Ed Koch never liked these panels, but they were a favorite of another three-term New York mayor, Robert F. Wagner, Jr. As his son Bobby once said to me, "My father had a committee for everything."

I'm with Mayor Wagner on this one. Here's how the blue ribbon panel works. There's an area of controversy in which something needs to be done. A couple of cops in town have been caught stealing, a couple of significant businesses have left your downtown, the U.S. Department of Interior has signaled that your town's historic landmark status is under review. You know something should be done, but it's complicated and one or more groups in town may have to endure more regulation. So what needs doing may be unwelcome at least to those groups.

What to do? You can spend the money to hire a consultant whose report will probably get picked apart, or you can form what the federal government likes to call "a stakeholders committee." At the local level these are also often called a "mayor's special committee."

These panels, working groups, committees, or some such generally come in two forms: those that run by Robert's Rules and those that run by consensus. After watching a few of these, I've come to prefer the consensus approach, although the other has its advantages. I like to say: "This committee is going to run like a church. The deacons are going to have to sit together until they reach consensus." And just when you think they can't, they do, and when they do you can say, taking cover, "Council is being cognizant of the advice given it by a committee of local people, all of whom have an interest in the matter, and who've studied it for months."

These committees should be large enough to include representatives of all the affected groups, yet not so large that the committee becomes unwieldy. Determining who should be included is something that is effectively done in open session with councilmembers rattling off interest groups. If someone legitimately complains he or she got left out, add the person later. If you wish to help shape the result, name the chairman yourself and make sure she's strong and shares your point of view. If you need to appear more even-handed, let the group choose its own chair.

Any good chairman will immediately ask for staff backup, so shortstop that by announcing at the committee's formation that the city staff, including the city attorney, will be available to the committee. Invite them to meet at city hall, and assign a council-member (preferably one who shares your point of view) to be the council liaison to the committee.

You should also "charge" the committee, which means that you write down in three or four sentences what the committee is supposed to be looking into and what it is expected to opine upon. You should formalize the committee by passing a resolution that includes the committee's composition and charge.

Give them a reasonable deadline. For policy-making recommendations, ninety days is generally adequate (you can always give extensions). Investigative committees will typically need more time. Ask for a written report of the committee's findings, including the committee's recommended changes of the existing law or policy. If consensus couldn't be reached, the disgruntled group may wish to file a minority report. There's no harm in that.

What is gained by forming a blue ribbon panel? First, the heat's off for at least ninety days, during which the government can legitimately say: "The status quo's in place as we await the findings of the Sullivan Committee." If the status quo isn't helpful to you in the short term, you can make temporary changes that, if they work, will become permanent changes by the time the committee renders its report.

If it happens that election day falls during the ninety days, all the better. Your opponent has very likely been deprived of an issue that could have been used against you. Keep election day in mind as you set the deadline, and make it 120 or 150 days if it's beneficial, but just because you have the Sullivan Committee's report a month before the election doesn't mean you have to go about implementing the committee's recommendations right away. Be statesmanlike and say: "This issue is too important to this community to get tangled up in election day politics. In fairness to the committee who has worked so hard, to the community and to my opponent, this looks like one for the January agenda."

What else has been gained from creating the panel? Most of the steam will have been drawn out of the interest groups at the committee level. Let them all harangue the committee. Better them than you. By the time they are back before you, their arguments will have been distilled and those who are angry with the committee's recommendations will be angry with the committee, not with you. In fact, they will be appealing to you to redress the wrongs perpetrated upon them by the committee. This is the typical post-committee dynamic: Those who came up short will appeal to you to overrule the committee, while those whose interests were served appeal to you to implement the committee's recommendations fully and promptly.

That's the worst case scenario, which isn't so bad. The best case scenario is that the committee, by taking the time to hear out all the interested parties, will actually have found common ground where there seemed to be none.

Of course savvy representatives of interest groups know how the committee game is played, and the most experienced of them may try to sidestep your process. If they try this trick, first, they'll try not to be named to the committee. If named, they won't go to the meetings. Or they'll just send a junior person to do reconnaissance. This "lay in the grass" approach is designed to position them so that they can discredit the committee's work when the findings are released, saying the committee's deliberations didn't include them. Then they'll petition the council to disregard the committee's work and fashion a "fair" policy or law, one that accommodates their interests in a way that is more to their liking.

Don't let this happen. If the committee chair tells you one of the groups isn't participating, write the group's leader a letter telling him where and when the next meeting is. Tell him to send a representative if he can't make it. If no one from the group shows, write their leader another letter telling him about the next meeting. This paper trail will come in handy when the group contests the committee's recommendations.

Besides saving a good many taxpayer dollars, what else has been gained? You've saved some time that can be used for governing. And meanwhile citizens have become involved with their government, and with you. They have been made to feel empowered. Panel members are generally leaders in their fields. Hopefully, they'll get a positive feeling about their local government from participating with it, and that feeling will get passed along to others in their field and with whom they associate. They may even get some press. In so doing, they get distantly associated with you, which is good for you. If their experience on the committee has been a generally positive one, it'll be harder for them to support your opponent next election day.

What's been lost? Not much. Certainly not your power. I would argue that it's been enhanced. If you've handled the committee's formation well at all, and whether you chose her or not, the chairman should call you up several times along the line and brief you on the committee's progress, its decision points, and the direction it's likely to be taking. The liaison should do the same thing. Here are opportunities for you to set the direction of the committee and influence its final report.

If you take half the steps suggested here, it is unlikely the committee's recommendations will be substantially at odds with those you have privately favored, but if they are (and there are occasional "runaway committees"), you can still just ditch the whole thing by putting it on the shelf. Or, if you don't like just a few of the committee's final recommendations, pick them apart at the council level until the interest groups are worn out. In the end all you have been given by the committee is the benefit of their collective advice. It is yours to take or reject.

Shortly after I first came onto the Beaufort City Council, there arose a controversy involving tourists and touring buses. In any town that is visited by large numbers of tourists (and it is estimated Beaufort now accommodates in excess of a million per year), there will be friction between the businesses that profit from tourism and the full-time residents who are inconvenienced by the tourists and the tourist service businesses. Over the past decade, the Beaufort City Council has probably spent more time fussing over our tourism ordinances than over any other section of the local code. There's money to be made by the operators, but apparently the size of the pie doesn't grow much from year to year. What varies is how it gets split, which is why the operators squabble so much over getting and defending their various territories.

Beaufort's tourists, like tourists everywhere, want to see the most expensive houses. These are largely antebellum buildings situated on the narrow and winding city streets of the neighborhood called The Point. A few could legitimately be called mansions. Others are precious two-hundred-year-old cottages. One favorite even dates back to the Indian Wars and is unique for the slits in its foundation that were designed for shooting muskets through. Scattered among this dignified collection of historical houses are a handful of churches and a four-city-block "main street" lined with commercial buildings that date from the same eras. All of this sits on a town plan that is the envy of the "new urbanists," a town plan that says "neighborhood" and means it. This was the place that had drawn me to Beaufort in 1988, the place where my now-former wife and I had decided we wanted to raise our family. It has drawn many others too. Its residents know they've got a good thing and they're fiercely unwilling to let it get away. So here you have sophisticated, resourceful, and motivated people who, as the numbers of tourists and tourist businesses increase, increasingly turn to the local government for the protection of their quality of life and their investments.

As the neighborhood where the rich people live, The Point calls forth some animosity from time to time. Close councilwatchers occasionally may even see this animosity revealed at the council level. I live on The Point, as does David Taub, my predecessor. In 1994 when the dispute began to unfold, the other three city council-members lived in other parts of the city. As the numbers of tourists and the numbers of residents' complaints grew, David knew the government would have to do something. There was an ordinance on the books regulating horse-carriage tours, but there was nothing about buses, kayaks, walking tours, vans, float boats, bicycles, snail trains, rickshaws, or any of the many other means of conveyance that the inventive minds of entrepreneurs can devise.

As a resident, I found the tour buses the most intrusive.

These are those huge Greyhound-sized buses that take on a load of passengers in, say, Charlotte, North Carolina, and set out for four days of sightseeing along the coasts of South Carolina and Georgia. They cruise into Beaufort for an hour and drive around The Point's narrow streets belching diesel fumes into front yards while thirty faces are lined up at the windows looking at you if you happen to be so unfortunate as to be anywhere in sight. On some tours the bus driver gets on the microphone and points out the sights. On the higher-end tours, a "step-on guide" boards the bus when it enters town and narrates the tour. Typically the passengers are fed box lunches. So while virtually no money is spent in Beaufort, The Point residents have been made to feel like monkeys in a zoo.

For years they complained to one another and to their government about the tour buses. Newly elected as a councilmember, I decided now was the time to get the buses off The Point. I suggested to David that a committee be formed, as committees had been formed many times before. At the next council meeting, Council deliberated over who should sit on the committee. Donnie Beer, who was very close with the chamber of commerce, insisted that the chamber play a key role. I insisted a resident of The Point be named. Council agreed with us both. A regional tourism development group called the Lowcountry Visitors Bureau facilitates the bus tours. Donnie wanted them on the committee. Council said fine. David proposed the Historic Beaufort Foundation, a nonprofit group that looks out for the interests of the historic district. Council said fine. Finally, I suggested Main Street Beaufort, a group that represents the interests of the property owners and business owners who conduct business in the historic district. Council agreed.

The city clerk sent out a letter to each of the five groups

inviting them to send a representative. Most of the representatives presented themselves to us at our next meeting. As I recall it, Cynthia Cole, then the executive director of the Historic Beaufort Foundation, asked most of the usual questions. Will the city staff the committee's meetings? What is the committee charged with doing? Is it written down somewhere? How much time do we have?

Then, and this is unusual, she asked, "Are we to run on Robert's Rules?" David, who was always very conscious of process, said, "We do and you should too." No one else said anything, and so it was decided. Suddenly a seriousness came over the committee, whose members were now in a bare knuckle competition to win the support of the swing vote, who would obviously be in this case Lise Sundrula, the director of the Main Street program.

David appointed Donnie the liaison to the committee and the meetings began. You could hear the screaming all over town. But the committee finally agreed on most issues, except the buses. There they were split and Lise was waffling. A tour bus operator in Savannah offered to take the committee and the city council on a tour of The Point to show them how nice one could be, and a tour was set up for one weekday midafternoon.

The favorite tourist route through The Point goes along the river where all the biggest houses are. It was therefore obvious where the tour would go. Well, as word of the tour got out, a few of my ever-resourceful neighbors temporarily parked their cars— legally of course—on the narrow streets of The Point so that the big bus would find it impossible to make the sharp turns. Sure enough, the tour was a fiasco, a delicious one. The bus was backing and filling and at one point it completely stalled as the well-meaning bus driver sought to maneuver his whale of a bus up those winding rocky creeks of streets. Under his breath he mut-

tered, "I've never seen cars parked in any of these places before . . ." but no matter. Main Street had the cover it needed to
cast its vote with the preservationists. That brought the matter
back to Council, which was as split on the buses as the committee had been. David and I were opposed to them. Donnie Beer
and Frank Glover favored them. That left Dr. Tony Bush, the defender of the small businessman, a gentle and generally very
quiet man, who often reminded me of Gregory Peck in *To Kill a
Mockingbird*.

The tour bus issue was one Tony struggled over, as he sought
to do what local governments do week after week: balance com-
peting interests. He had not been on the bus ride, but he had
heard about it.

In the end Tony was persuaded by Main Street's position.
They were the representatives of small business on the committee. Main Street's position gave Tony cover from the small business owners to whose interests he was sympathetic, as did the
committee's report. If a bus tour operator came to him, he could
say: "Well, you were represented on the committee by the Lowcountry Visitors Bureau and this is what the committee recommended. Even Main Street wants this, and they represent the
heart and soul of the business community. I was just doing what
the committee suggested." So he voted with David and me, and
the buses were history.

23. Counterpunching

PART of public life is keeping your feet under you when you are attacked. No matter how hard you try to build consensus, and you should try very hard, there is no significant step you will take that will not draw criticism. Being attacked in the press is a fact of public life. What it says is that you are somebody and you are doing something. Still, only the most combative of elected officials actually enjoy the give and take on page one, and many dread it.

The most important question to ask when you are attacked is, "Who is the attacker and what is his credibility?" You have been elected. On election day you were the candidate most of the voters preferred. That means you have substantial credibility. Because you have credibility, paradoxically you can make your opponents credible. So be wary of elevating nuts on the fringe. By engaging in a public debate with someone heretofore unknown, you can make them known—known for disagreeing with you. Is that good for you in the long term? Probably not. Clearly, then, sometimes discretion is the better part of valor.

When I first heard of Reverend Al Sharpton (who, as this book was being written, was running for President), he was a guy who couldn't get five people together to lie in with him at a subway station. But he could call names, and he did. After a little while, the taunting got under Ed Koch's skin and Ed started defending himself. He started attacking back. "I'm not a punching bag," he'd say, "I punch back!" Then he'd walk out under the lights and let someone have it. Well, every time Ed punched Al Sharpton back, he made Sharpton a little bigger, so that after a year or so there were hundreds of people with Sharpton. They marched across the Brooklyn Bridge. They picketed city hall. Sharpton was on the radio. He was on TV. Pretty soon his name was a household word. I do not mean to convey that Sharpton might not have become famous anyway because he is a man with many talents, including tenacity and courage. I mean that by calling Sharpton names, Ed helped him get started.

So it is a mistake to help nobodies who are unfriendly to you become somebodies. That means sometimes you have to just take a punch. Most of the time, however, the right thing's to counterpunch. Here's how.

Cool down. If you think the attack's really unfair and you want to really let them have it back with both barrels, write your reply and put it in your desk drawer for a couple of days. Then go back to it and see how it sounds. Read it to someone you trust. If it could sound shrill to the casual newspaper reader, tone it down. Keep in mind that letters carry a heavier punch when they appear on newsprint than on your computer screen. You can't hit the delete button there either.

Keep your letter as short as possible. Effective letters generally don't run past 250 words. Why? Because readers don't read long letters. So for every twenty-five words you write, you're losing 10 percent of your audience. Consider cutting out the first couple of paragraphs as you set the stage for your main point. The short zinger's the best because it's readable and memorable.

Begin your letter by repeating in your own words the charge

against you. Don't try to answer every charge. Pick out the one you can deal with best. But if one charge is important and the rest are fluff, make sure to answer the important charge.

Confine your comments to policy. Do not attack character. Ad hominem attacks are virtually always counterproductive.

As soon as you have a letter that's strong, considered, and temperate in tone, send it in. The sooner you get your letter in the less time your attacker's letter has to get traction.

Defending yourself's fine. Having others come to your defense is even better. This is where knowing every inch of your community really helps. If there's someone who feels strongly on your behalf, get that person to write the letter. Or write the letter yourself but get him to sign it as his own.

In early 2003, a controversy arose regarding the siting of a new high school in the northern part of Beaufort County. The city didn't want the school to be as far from the city as the school board proposed because that would mean extending sewer beyond the city's and county's agreed upon plan. The city counterproposed that the school be sited closer to Beaufort next to two other schools and about a mile from the Marine Corps Air Station, Beaufort, a U.S. Marine Corps/U.S. Navy jet fighter facility.

The head of the school district's facilities committee at the time was retired Brigadier General Steve Cheney. After taking the look at running for Congress, Cheney ran unsuccessfully in 2002 for a South Carolina House seat, and by 2003 he was at the Beaufort County School District as the chairman of their facilities committee, an honorary position. Correctly perceiving the need for political cover, the school district had set up this committee to take the heat for the siting of the new schools, and, good soldier that he is, Cheney had waded into the fight on their behalf.

Trying to round up some support for their 1970s-style sprawl plan of building the new high school out in the middle of some tomato fields, in February 2003 the facilities committee called a public meeting at which they trotted out all the reasons why the school should go in the relative middle of nowhere. There Cheney brought up base closures, and suggested that siting the school near the base, as was being proposed by the city and county, would imperil the base as it went forward toward the promised 2005 Base Realignment and Closure (BRAC) process. Cheney was correct in observing that low-flying jets and big schools are generally to be kept apart. However, he hadn't done his homework on this particular situation. Cheney's charge sent the city and county scurrying back to the base's planner who once again, citing the directions of the runways and the air traffic patterns, said he had reviewed the alternatives and in his opinion neither site encroached upon the base.

Several weeks later a zoning change that would enable the school district to site the school in the tomato fields came up for review by the county's land use committee, chaired by W. R. "Skeet" Von Harten, a retired Marine Corps lieutenant colonel, a former chairman of the chamber of commerce's military enhancement committee whose job it is to lobby Washington to keep Beaufort's military bases open, a former county council chairman, and in 2003 the vice chairman of the county council. The Von Hartens go back many years in Beaufort as mechanics, builders, and shrimpers. As a group they are tough guys, and Skeet's as tough as any of them. A great big blond guy with a direct manner, and a love of the limelight, he is the very picture of a local official.

At the zoning meeting, the committee, under Von Harten's direction, denied the zoning change. The denial apparently angered Cheney, because a week or so later he wrote a letter to the paper that attacked both Skeet and me. The letter said we, on behalf of the county and the city, were imperiling the future of the air base.

In attacking me, Cheney reached back to a three-year-old letter signed by me as mayor in which the city asked the Navy not to relocate its Super Hornet jets to Beaufort's air station, saying (according to the Navy's Environmental Impact Statement) they would create thunderstorm noise virtually around the clock, thus generating so many noise complaints that people would begin calling for the base to be closed. In his letter Cheney argued the alternative: that by trying to keep the Super Hornets out we were actually endangering the base's future.

In the same letter Cheney attacked Skeet for trying to move the high school closer to the base and thereby imperiling its future operations by fostering encroachment of its air space.

The attack made Skeet hopping mad. He had done his homework, worked hard on the base, and was committed to keeping it viable in Beaufort. Because Cheney's not nobody, I knew I would have to respond as well.

I let a couple of days go by and then I called Skeet up. He was in the middle of writing his response. He said he was working on the Super Hornets. I found that interesting because he hadn't been attacked on the jets, he'd been attacked on his committee's denial of the zoning change. I was the one Cheney had attacked on the jets. But it gave me an idea. And I said it right then. "Good," I said. "You take the Super Hornets and I'll take the school." The result was that Skeet's letter defended me and my letter defended Skeet.

Well, everyone loved the letters, and the way we tag-teamed Cheney. The general didn't answer either letter. No one else did either.

It is worth noting in conclusion that the longer you serve and the more you are attacked, the more used to it you become. In this exchange I never got angry at all. And I would have five years ago. I simply saw it as an opportunity to make my points again, an opportunity to seek to move public opinion.

Answering the general's letter was also an opportunity to subtly make the point again, as I had been taught by Ed, that "I'm not a punching bag. I punch back!" If your opponents know you'll be going after them, they'll think twice before they go after you.

I would also guess that the next time Cheney decides to attack a couple of big dogs, he'll take them on one at a time.

24. Taking Credit

WHILE you are in office, there will very likely be several reporters who will be assigned to cover the local beat, each for a year or two at a time. These reporters generally know nothing about who did what before they got there. They only know what they are told about it by you and others who were there. It is unlikely they will go back to old newspapers, although there may be extensive clip files at their offices. It is even more unlikely they will go back and dig up the minutes of past public meetings. In a very unusual circumstance someone may show them an old clipping or even the minutes of a past meeting, but such instances will be rare. The new reporters' editors are overworked and underpaid and her predecessors left without leaving forwarding addresses.

A short institutional memory is the nature of the press. Therefore it is worthwhile to give a history lesson to each new reporter about what you have done. This meeting can be scheduled comfortably under the heading of "getting to know you" and talking about yours and the town's priorities for a new reporter on the beat. However the what-you-have-done part is far more important to you than the what-you-will-do part.

Formal priorities mostly get in the way. The victories you will score will be mostly from converting unforeseen opportunities. A few will be the result of multiyear sieges. A formal list of your ten top goals for next year, if you have such a thing and have made them public, will more often than not only set up next year's failed report card, if it is graded seriously.

The arrival of each new reporter is a chance to rewrite history a little bit. Some politicians are brilliant at this. Gerald Ford, who ran a status quo White House, has tried to convince us that he set the stage for Reagan's successes. Jimmy Carter, voted out of office for botching the Iranian hostage crisis, turned to peace as an ex-president and has now won a Nobel Prize for helping settle conflicts around the globe. Those who play this game and win are not the shrinking violet types. Others, those who are inclined to underplay their own achievements, will soon see their role in those achievements buried by the more aggressive rewriters.

Delicate balance, and patience, is required because reporters as a group are not fools and you are not their only source. They will be speaking with your detractors as well. Philosophers may argue over whether it is better to have done the thing and not received sufficient credit, or to have had a small role and received most of the credit. Politicians, who must keep at least one eye on their prospects in the next election, know the answer: the credit's the thing.

It isn't easy to shape the account of history so that it shows you at your best, and there are pitfalls along the way. In the 2000 presidential campaign, clever imagists in George W. Bush's camp took Al Gore's comment that he had "invented the Internet" and hung it around his neck. Given the closeness of the race, it can be argued that that overreach cost Gore the presidency. The vice president had undoubtedly not intended his comment to be taken literally when he said it, but Bush's handlers succeeded in making Gore look like a boastful "politician" by pulling this bit of hyperbole out of context and sticking it in the headlines.

The classic line in the area of taking credit is: "If something good happens on my watch, I should get the credit. If the opposite (a bad thing) had happened, I would have gotten the blame, right?" Okay, so then the question becomes what does "on my watch" mean? In the case of an official who has held office, at the minimum it means something he or she has voted "yes" on. If you vote against taking over the cable TV utility and the "ayes" have it, and the public utility turns out to deliver more channels for less than the for-profit entity did, and it makes money for the city, you will run a risk when you try to take credit for the public utility's success.

It's surprising how little homework actually gets done in politics, so it should not be surprising how often politicians are permitted to take liberties with the truth. Tim Russert of *Meet the Press*, who has distinguished himself as a talk-show host who actually does his homework, began his career working for then New York Senator Daniel Patrick Moynihan.

In 1982 a Long Island congressman named Bruce Caputo decided to challenge Moynihan. Caputo was apparently uncomfortable about his lack of service to the military, so as he moved up in public life, he fabricated a service record and then embellished it. As those who traffic in untruths will, the more he described his military service, the more glamorous it became. Russert, then just out of law school, did just what a good campaign staffer should do—he went out and learned as much as he could about his boss's opponent. As he read through the various newspaper profiles and official biographies, his nose told him there was something fishy about Caputo's service record. There were just too many versions.

In the spring of 1982, with Caputo unchallenged in the May GOP primary, Russert happened to be having a cup of coffee with a *Daily News* reporter and an Associated Press reporter, and they mentioned they'd be having lunch with the congressman later that day.

Russert said: "Ask him for his serial number."

It wasn't a big deal, but the reporters remembered what Tim had said. At lunch, speaking for the record of his record, Caputo happened to mention that he'd been a "McNamara whiz kid," meaning that he'd served in the Pentagon under Defense Secretary Robert McNamara during the Kennedy Administration. McNamara's Pentagon staff is recalled in Washington as a group that brought modern business techniques and sophistication into a military establishment that hadn't changed much since World War II nearly a generation before.

This comment by Caputo, coupled with Russert's comment, prompted the reporters to make the requisite phone calls to check out the congressman's service record. A week later the story of his phony service record hit the papers and he withdrew from the race. That set up a Republican primary free-for-all between three GOP also-rans, and the table was set for a Moynihan reelection cakewalk. These are the episodes that turn lowly staffers into legends.

It is not a good idea to take credit for something you have not by any stretch done. There is always a chance there will be a young Tim Russert on your opponent's team. It is better to have played a modest role in many things, and then, when one of them turns out spectacularly well, you, over time, make more and more of your contribution. This technique was used to great effect by former Beaufort Mayor Henry Chambers.

In Beaufort there is a city park down by the river that is beloved by all of us in town, known officially as the Henry C. Chambers Waterfront Park. Twenty-five years into its life, the park is experiencing structural problems, problems the city will spend millions over the next few years trying to solve. So it can be fairly said, as I write this chapter, that I know more than I would like to know about this park.

Beaufort is a Marine Corps town. The Marine Corps recruit depot at Parris Island has been training Marine Corps recruits on a continuous basis since 1915. A landing strip in the Burton section of Beaufort has served as a Marine Corps air station since 1960.

Parris Island has long had a very good band that plays at the recruit graduations. In the years between the world wars, the band played on the Beaufort Courthouse steps on occasional Saturday nights. The whole town came and spread their blankets on the courthouse lawn or on the bluff across the street that overlooks the river and enjoyed the music.

After World War II, Beaufort's population swelled and the courthouse lawn was soon too small for the concerts. In 1950 the need for a new performance space was seen by Mayor Angus Fordham who went to work on the problem. Fordham and his council identified an unused section of mudflats behind a gas station along the Beaufort waterfront, and arranged for the city to float a $50,000 bond to pay for a watertight bulkhead around the perimeter of the area (about 2.5 acres) to be filled, and then fill in the area with mud dredged from the Beaufort River. In classic old Beaufort fashion, the Marines contributed half a quonset hut that served as the park's bandshell. Fordham christened the place Freedom Mall. The Parris Island Band played the opener, and the new park was a hit.

Freedom Mall was such a big hit, in fact, that Mayor Fordham and the city fathers soon cast their collective eye down the city's waterfront from there to the bridge that connects Beaufort to

Lady's Island. The bridge is about four city blocks to the east of Freedom Mall. What they saw on those four waterfront blocks was a sorry collection of dilapidated docks and wharves whose pilings stuck out of the mud at low tide.

Wouldn't it be great, they thought, if Freedom Mall could be extended the four blocks to the bridge? Instead of a crummy old underutilized waterfront, the city would have several more blocks upon which to build stores, a new perimeter street to improve the downtown grid and circulation and parking.

The effort to fill in the waterfront was a more complicated project than Freedom Mall because it required the acquisition of the portions of the lots that were under the docks, the riparian rights to which were owned by several dozen individuals. So Mayor Fordham and Council set about convincing the property owners that the value of their street frontage lots would be substantially enhanced after they sold their back river frontage lots to the city and the city improved them. This they began to undertake in 1959.

Having set the table in preparation for the project, Fordham stepped down three years later after seventeen years as mayor. He was succeeded as mayor by his "understudy" on Council, a banker named Willie Scheper who served from 1963 to 1967. The waterfront expansion project languished during the good times that were the Scheper years.

Scheper was followed into the center chair at council meetings by one Monroe Key, a tall, lean, good-looking businessman from the Carolina upcountry. A successful manager with a track record with Mr. Edward Kronsberg, the owner of the Edward's 5 & 10¢ Store chain, Key had been moved to Beaufort to manage the Bay Street store, a fixture of the downtown Beaufort shopping district at that time. As a merchant himself, Key understood the "main street" merchants who didn't want to create a new "main street" on the waterfront one block away. They did, however, want to get rid of the dilapidated wharves, and they wanted more parking. It was Key who proposed and popularized the notion of a Freedom Mall extension with a parking lot at each end, and it was he who finally convinced the property owners to sell. While the paperwork was not done when Key was transferred out of Beaufort by Mr. Kronsberg, the public good that the park would do for Beaufort had been shown by Key and the project was ready to be brought to fruition.

Into that situation in 1970 came young Henry C. Chambers, a political newcomer running for the mayor's seat just vacated by Key. Returning home from Clemson University, Chambers had gone into the concrete business, and with steel reinforced concrete the new fashion in construction in the late '60s, his business, Burton Block, was thriving. Big, broad-shouldered, and with a booming voice, Chambers was born for the political life. He loved the intrigues, the risks, the illusions, and the possibilities of politics, and even the controversy. He was so comfortable in controversy, in fact, he sometimes created it unnecessarily. There was no jam so tight that Henry couldn't talk his way out of it, or at least so it appeared. Beaufort loved Henry Chambers. He was a go-getter, and they elected him their mayor.

Chambers recognized immediately the possibilities of the Freedom Mall extension. It was a project ready to be built, and he was a builder. As a builder, Chambers sold Council on a more modern design: near the old shoreline where the depths were modest, some poured concrete bulkheading and fill should be used, he said. Beyond that bulkhead he proposed an elaborate series of steel reinforced concrete decks, wells, and walls resting on poured concrete pilings and footings. The new park plan in-

cluded a promenade, an amphitheater, a marina, and a great
lawn. In the Chambers plan, as in the Key plan, Fordham's Freedom Mall became a parking lot.

When the bids were opened, the low bidder was Burton
Block, the mayor's company. The city's documents that memori-
alize this 1971–72 process and the ensuing contract and change
orders with Burton Block are sketchy, but according to the recol-
lections of participants the cost of the Freedom Mall extension
project was about $2.5 million. The city's entire annual budget
was only in the hundreds of thousands of dollars. No problem,
said the can-do mayor. Turning to an eminent member of the
Clemson network, Senator Strom Thurmond, who had by then
been in the U.S. Senate for twenty years, Chambers sought, and
received, federal money for the park, lots of it.

The senator attended the park's 1973 dedication, the ceremony at which the park was christened "the Henry C. Chambers
Waterfront Park." From there Henry, who as mayor was perfectly
positioned to do so, set himself up as the expert on the park, its
design, maintenance, and uses. Moreover, and brilliantly, he got
the state highway department to make and locate a dozen or
so large directional signs that directed motorists to the Henry
C. Chambers Waterfront Park from every major intersection in
town.

When I came to town in 1988, fifteen years after the park's
christening, Chambers was still mayor and it was customary to
hear him described as a visionary. The visionary reference was always to the same project, the park. Newspaper stories about the
park, and Chambers, all followed suit.

So it was that over twenty-five years Henry Chambers re-
wrote history to make himself not just the builder of the park,
but its father as well. The contributions of Fordham and Key and

their councils were all but forgotten, and I'd have never known of them at all had I not been ringing doorbells in my 1997 council-manic reelection campaign when I came up on the Mossy Oaks doorstep of Angus Fordham's sister, then in her eighties. She asked me in, and, contrary to my usual practice, I accepted her offer. Over a glass of sweet tea she told me this story, a story I later confirmed with several other old-timers around town who were in positions, as the park decisions were made, to know.

25. Dancing with the Wolves

IN Washington it is said, "If you want a friend in Washington, get a dog."

There are generally no faithful friendships among politicians. There are only alliances. And alliances shift. Elections come around regularly and over time, if you are fortunate, you will find yourself surrounded by politicians you have beaten in one race or another. You may have forgiven them for running against you—although that is unlikely—but it is a sure thing that they will not have forgiven you for beating them.

Ed Koch used to say to me, mostly when Mario Cuomo's name would come up: "You never really forgive the people you've run against. There is always something that happened in the campaign that you just can't get over." It all began when they ran against each other for mayor in 1977 and Ed won. Cuomo's people had put up signs at subway stops that said "Vote for Cuomo, Not the Homo." And when Mario had been asked about it, he didn't chastise his people. He shrugged it off.

Ed never forgave Mario for the signs. And very reasonably. But if it hadn't been for the signs, it would very likely have been something else.

Signs or no signs, Ed beat Mario in 1977, and he beat five other hopefuls too. One of those was Herman Badillo, a congressman from the Bronx and a former Bronx borough president. When Ed set up his government in anticipation of taking office in

January 1978, he reached out to a number of groups. In the context of the racial politics that so dominate New York, and given his tight margin of victory, Ed chose for deputy mayors an African American, a Hispanic, an Italian American, and a woman. He invited Herman Badillo to fill the Hispanic slot and to Ed's surprise Herman agreed. Herman was the only one of his former primary opponents that Ed invited in.

From the beginning it was unclear just exactly what Herman's job in the new government was. But he built up a big staff and he attended a lot of functions. In his mind he was probably licking his wounds and mending his fences while waiting for the next political opportunity to come along. Not surprisingly, that didn't suit Ed, who wanted Herman and his staff to actually do some real work.

It wasn't long into 1978 when the matter of trying to reverse the decline of the South Bronx came up on the Koch Administration's radar screen. Landlords were walking away from their buildings and the blight was spreading. Whole blocks were left to deteriorate. The area is in the vicinity of Yankee Stadium, and when the Yankees were playing in the World Series, one of the buildings nearby caught fire. Between innings the TV cameras would pan over to the fire, which was seeming to be left to burn out of control, and suddenly the city's supposed neglect of the South Bronx was a national issue. President Jimmy Carter came to the city soon after that to tour the area and pledge support. Bobby Wagner at the city planning commission took on the issue and with the commission staff's help he formulated a revitalization plan that called for local, state, and federal money, lots of it.

Herman was put in charge of implementing the city's plan. He was the obvious choice, if he was to do anything at all as deputy mayor. Always territorial and prickly, Herman never liked the Wagner Plan (mostly because it wasn't the Badillo Plan) and so, in seeking to get it implemented, he just went through the motions, failing to line up the votes to get the city's portion of the money from the city's board of estimate, for example. If the city wasn't willing to put up its own money, how could the state and the feds be expected to participate?

As the vote neared and it became increasingly clear that several members of the board of estimate, most notably City Controller Jay Goldin with two votes, would not be voting in favor of the measure, Herman racheted up his rhetoric. Belatedly he had come to the conclusion that he needed this one. But Goldin and others were by that time lost to him. Then Herman called them names and the whole messy spectacle was played out on the front pages of the papers.

Quite reasonably, Goldin called up Ed and asked him bluntly to get his deputy mayor under control. Ed's response was surprising. He said: "No. Herman has an independent constituency. He's entitled to protect it. If that means speaking freely, I won't seek to stop him from doing that."

Goldin responded, "Well, how would you like it if my deputy, Marty Ives, was attacking you and I said well, he can do as he pleases?"

Ed said: "That's different. Marty Ives doesn't have an independent constituency."

While a huge opportunity for the South Bronx was lost that day, and wounds were inflicted that haven't healed to this day, the way the blame was apportioned by the reporters covering the story was very, very interesting. The revitalization of the South Bronx, one would have concluded from reading the papers, fell apart because of squabbling between Badillo and Goldin, and Koch was above the fray. Additionally, Badillo didn't attack Koch at all, and neither did Goldin. In this way Ed managed to avoid the blame for a huge failure early in his first term. (In Ed's third term the city created a ten-year plan that ultimately built 150,000 housing units in the South Bronx at the cost of $5.1 billion.)

Abe Lincoln did a very similar thing in 1864 with Salmon P. Chase, the former senator from Ohio who was Lincoln's secretary of the treasury. As the 1864 election approached and the war effort yielded more disappointing results, Chase took to being increasingly critical of Lincoln. "Why hasn't the president yet freed the slaves?" Chase asked repeatedly. To Lincoln it was apparently obvious that Chase wanted to get himself fired so that he could turn around and run in the Republican primary against and to the left of Lincoln. Lincoln simply ignored the attacks and declined to remove Chase and after a few months the crisis had passed. It was too late for Chase to mount a campaign. So he went to the Supreme Court instead.

With the benefit of these two examples before me, I faced a similar challenge in 2000. Here's what happened.

Donnie Beer had to resign her councilmanic seat in 1999 to run for mayor. When I resigned my councilmanic seat to be sworn in as mayor, Donnie announced she would run for my old seat and she won. As soon as she was sworn back in as a city council-member, the council elected her its mayor pro tempore. Now I had sitting next to me someone who quite clearly would prefer to be mayor. And, because we had run for a seventeen-month term, I had a reelection campaign coming up in about a year. Moreover, I was in the midst of a messy divorce and custody battle.

Right off the bat Donnie started saying the Waterfront Park was falling apart and the city wasn't doing anything about it. She was right. But there was a good reason. The city was just then finishing up the rebuilding of all the streets and sidewalks in its core commercial historic downtown area and that "streetscape" project was sapping all our extra energies and resources. Clearly we would next be turning to the park. My thought was we'd form some parks committees and put Donnie on all the committees and by the time the committees deliberated and the results of their deliberations were brought before Council, the election would be over and Streetscape would be over too. Then the time would be right to turn to the park.

At the same time, Donnie started making comments about how the city wasn't doing enough to help poor people in the historic district fix up their houses. In previous years as a councilman I had done quite a bit of work helping poor people get Community Development Block Grant (CDBG) money to fix up their houses, so I knew how labor intensive that job is. Each house presents a unique set of financing and construction problems. It's a governmental quagmire and I was delighted she wanted to wade into it. We set up another committee to work on that and put her on it.

It was the Herman Badillo plan all over again. Now if she wanted to be critical of the park, I could say, "Well you're running the committee, why haven't you done more?" If she wanted to say we weren't doing enough to rehabilitate poor people's houses, I could say: "Well your committee needs to get on the stick and bring some recommendations back to Council. That's what's holding things up."

She didn't run against me. No one did. And she didn't say any of those things. Instead Donnie has worked very hard on both the park and improving housing conditions and she has made good things happen in both areas.

PART THREE

Losing Power

26. Scandal

ABOUT two o'clock in the morning on January 10, 1986, I was awakened at my apartment in Greenwich Village by a phone call from the police desk at city hall. The duty officer said to me that Queens Borough President Donald Manes had been found bleeding in his car alongside the Brooklyn-Queens Expressway and that he had been taken to Booth Memorial Medical Center Hospital in Flushing, Queens.

I rode out to the hospital with Ed a half-hour later. It was apparent from the doctor's description of Donny's condition that Donny had tried to take his own life. It was likewise apparent that he would have succeeded had not an alert police officer, thinking he was helping a motorist in distress, pulled up behind Donny's car moments after Donny had cut himself. The doctor said Donny had lost more than a third of his blood.

Neither Ed nor I had the slightest idea what had prompted Donny Manes to try to kill himself. Marlene Manes, Donny's shocked and distraught wife, predictably offered no explanation for Donny's behavior either. As Ed and I rode back to Manhattan in the darkness before dawn, we sat in silence confronted by the mystery.

We did not have to wait very long before the pieces began falling together. That night was the beginning of a two-year period during which the reporters that covered city hall essentially threw away the press releases issued by my office as they pursued the story their readers wanted to read: scandal at city hall.

The prosecutors now controlled what went on the front pages and when. In the end it was shown that Ed Koch had personally had nothing to do with any corrupt activities, and that he had done everything he could have done to root out the corruption once it was discovered. But he was tarred anyway. We all were.

Life in a city hall beset by scandal is a singular experience. But it is not an unusual one. With power, regrettably, sometimes comes the abuse of power, and from that inevitably comes scandal. Scandal, like all else in public life, can be managed. What it was and how it was managed will determine how great was the political damage, how severe was the loss of power. For as surely as you gained power, you will lose it, whether by scandal, illness, misjudgments, or simply because you have held it long enough.

Many have been in storms, but few have been in two converging category five hurricanes. That was the situation created by the 1985 parking violations bureau scandal and the Bess Mess, both being prosecuted by U.S. Attorney Rudolf Giuliani, who had obviously read the Thomas E. Dewey playbook. With John Gotti, the Dapper Don, under his belt, he was gaining momentum for his eventual run for mayor and beyond. And this with four daily newspapers, a notorious muckraking weekly, two round-the-clock all-news radio stations, and six local TV stations tracking the disclosures. Here's what I learned.

There is an end. When the scandal is unfolding around you—today's unthinkable revelation piled upon yesterday's seismic explosion—in your exasperation you will legitimately wonder whether the surprises will ever stop. They will. The prosecutor's job is to build the maximum pressure so as to "turn" key people into witnesses against you. You, or whoever is the biggest fish in the pond, are the one the prosecutor wants. This isn't paranoid, it's elementary public relations for prosecutors. Corrupt health inspectors get little headlines, but corrupt mayors get big headlines, lots of them. Thus it is important to remember that there is nothing random or haphazard about the ways the scandal stories unfold. They are being carefully choreographed by the prosecutor's office so as to put maximum pressure on those who might know something. The prosecutor's office will deny that there are leaks. It's nonsense. Who else is leaking? Those being investigated? Who will investigate the illegal leaks? Not the prosecutor's office. When everything they have to reveal has been revealed, the story will die down at least until the courtroom stories start.

Get out of city hall. You may have become accustomed to friendly handshakes and sincere applause. Perhaps in the good times you came to take these niceties for granted. You are accustomed no more. Actively seek them out. A friendly handshake and a nice round of applause will never feel or sound so sweet as at your first public appearance after the scandal hits the front page. The public you see face-to-face will be the last to desert you. Go get this nourishment, and keep going back.

Don't get ahead of the story. The prosecutor may know where the story's headed, but you don't. So don't speculate with reporters. In particular, resist responding to hypothetical questions. (Hypothetical questions are questions that start with "if.") Just say: "That's a hypothetical question. If what you imagine ever actually comes to pass, I'll evaluate the whole situation at that time and then maybe I'll have an answer to that question." If you speculate, the next revelation from the prosecutor's office will be precisely the one that will make you look worst. One of prosecutors' favorite techniques is to "float" their theories by getting the most aggressive reporters to ask you to respond to unattributed quotes. Don't respond to comments that are not sourced. Instead say something like: "If you can't tell me who said that, I will have to assume it came from someone who doesn't know what they're talking about. Why should I lend their theory a credibility that at this moment it obviously doesn't have?"

There's responsibility and then there's responsibility. You are accountable for everything that happens within your government. But if something happens that was purposely concealed from you by a corrupt or several corrupt people, you should be just as outraged by it as the public is.

Don't be defensive. Don't rest until you get all the facts. When the situation warrants it, throw the book at the wrongdoers. Put them on immediate leave as soon as you have probable cause.

Never cover up. Nine times out of ten it's the cover-up, more than the crime, that causes the permanent political injury.

You know on day one of the scandal what you knew and when you knew it. If you are 100 percent clean, you can be your own spokesperson. If you may have a problem, get a lawyer to talk for you. You are much more likely to survive politically if you don't get caught lying. A sudden spate of "no comments" is almost as bad. So day one's important. The sudden appearance of your lawyer speaking for you a month into the scandal makes you look guilty. A lawyer speaking for you on day one looks better. Say: "This is a legal matter and there's no one who wants to see it resolved more than me. That's why I've put Learned Hand Henderson here on the case. If you have any questions, he'll be in a position to answer them for you," and then turn it over to him for good.

Resist the temptation to get the government to pay your lawyer. If the government pays your lawyer, then the client is the government. That means just when you need Henderson the most (when your interests diverge from the government's), you will find that he cannot be there for you. The government ought to have a lawyer protecting its interests—as for example when you decide to put the alleged wrongdoers on leave—and the government's lawyer's work can save your lawyer some time and that can save you some money. So be sure to choose for your lawyer someone who can work with the government's lawyer.

Try not to take things personally. Both the prosecutor and the reporters are doing what they are being paid to do. If they do it well, as Rudy Giuliani and a whole host of reporters did in 1985 and 1986, they will make their reputations here. You shouldn't be trying to help them succeed in gutting you, but neither should you view their efforts as a vendetta directed at you. If you succeed in coming through the gauntlet with good humor, two things will happen. The reporters will have gone somewhat easier on you because you didn't act guilty, and you will have earned their respect for being a hardened pro—a respect that will have lasting value once the crisis has passed. Keep in mind that the end of the scandal is very likely not an end in any real sense: hopefully you will still be in office, many of the same reporters will still be covering you, and election day will be approaching.

Don't give an inch. If before you would have called a reporter and complained about her story, call her now. If you would have kidded her in a council meeting, kid her. If you would have complained to her editor, complain. If you would have demanded a correction, demand it now. Not only will the reporters continue to respect you and know that they cannot abuse you, but they will also perceive that you're still the old you and not dispirited by the scandal or, worse yet, guilty of something and therefore hiding from them.

Finally, keep doing the job—even if you cannot get the news of your achievements into the paper. Here's your mindset. This is going to be over. I may be weakened somewhat by the taint of scandal. But I'm still the incumbent. And I'm up for reelection in a year-and-a-half. I'm going to need to tell the voters all the things I did for them in this term. I'd better build a record of achievement or one of those rats in the prosecutor's office will get it into his pinhead to run against me!

27. Running from Behind

ED used to say: "I don't mind making enemies. I just worry that at the wrong time they might all get together."

Despite the structural advantages of incumbency, there are times—such as during a scandal or economic downturn—when the incumbent must run from behind, sometimes from way behind. An incumbent running from behind necessarily runs a very different kind of campaign than most. All things that are strong about such campaigns derive from the fact that the incumbent has been there. He can raise the money he needs because he's been there. He knows upon whom he can rely because he and his team have been there together. He knows the issues because he's been there.

What's weak about these campaigns likewise derives from the fact that the incumbent has been there. He can't generate Camelot-style excitement, because the electorate's heard his life's story, and his family's, and they're tired of both of them. From previous campaigns he has entrenched adversaries, sometimes powerful ones. And because of previous statements and legislative actions, he may also be pinned down on several of the major issues, probably even pinned down in unpopular positions.

How do you make lemonade from these lemons? Go back to the basics. Take a poll. Find from it a new issue that shows promise and can serve as a diversion from the mistakes of the past. Meanwhile shift (where possible) the blame for your past mistakes to the state or county, or wherever else is available. Make the new campaign a new beginning.

Use your organization to out-organize your opponent by getting signs in yards, and identifying your voters and getting them to the polls.

The classic example of an incumbent's successful run from behind is New York Mayor Robert Wagner's run for a third term in 1961. When Wagner was first elected in 1953, and when he ran for reelection in 1957, he had been supported by what was then known as the Democratic party regular organization, sometimes also known with either fear or derision as The Tammany Hall Machine. By 1960, however, Wagner was seen as vulnerable, even by his own people.

Wagner's second term had been marred by a series of agency-level scandals: corruption in the buildings department, at the fire department, at purchasing, and at school construction. No one said Wagner was personally corrupt, but he was widely faulted for not moving strongly enough to root corruption out of the government. As he approached reelection, the *Times* opined the Wagner Administration "had run badly downhill."

At the same time, the head of the regular organization, Carmine DeSapio, was openly looking for a replacement for Wagner. DeSapio saw Wagner as beatable. Carmine had only one agenda item: he didn't want to hang with a loser. So, after promising him Tammany's support, he brought State Controller Arthur Leavitt into the race.

At the outset of the '61 campaign, Wagner artfully shifted his field, blaming the scandals on DeSapio and the corrupting influence upon city government of DeSapio's organization. If he was reelected, Wagner said, he'd sweep Tammany Hall out of the city government. And he knew just where to sweep, he added.

It turned out his timing was superb. With the support of President Kennedy and the commitment to reform that the White House's support implied, Wagner in just a few months built a new coalition in New York. The Democratic party's reform clubs fell in behind him one by one. Surprisingly, and as a further tribute to Wagner's political acumen, many of the city's unions did the same. Thus, in the rank and file of the city government Wagner found a political organization. On primary day he swept virtually every election precinct. Overnight Tammany was out and the reformers were in.

If 1960 was the first presidential election in which television played a significant role, likewise 1961 was the first New York City mayoral election in which television swung votes in large blocs. In 1960 Kennedy appeared youthful, vital, thoughtful, and idealistic next to the pasty-faced and pragmatic Nixon. In 1961 neither Wagner nor Levitt were matinee idols, but Wagner's muckraking message, and the intensity with which he delivered it, were made for TV. Already TV's unmatched ability to seem to reveal the person inside the candidate was influencing election results.

Wagner had run against himself and won overwhelmingly.

The same can be done in town politics. To survive changing times and multiple elections, you must approach each election with a fresh eye. Reinvent yourself. Don't worry about your past. An incumbent's past is only as harmful as she makes it seem to her constituents as she seeks to apologize for it. So don't apologize. Look forward instead. Alliances shift. The task before you is to form a winning coalition from whatever quarters are available to you before election day.

28. Elder Statesman

YOU bet the long shot and lost. It was yours . . . until it got away. Or you got out gracefully. It happens to us all. You're out. Now what?

Avoid bitterness, be magnanimous about your successor—at least for a few months—and make up with your enemies. Being an elder statesman is a new role, to be sure, but you can learn to play it and make it work for you.

Those things you came into government to do you may find in time can still be done. There is political life after political death. I know this is counterintuitive, but in some ways you now have more power.

Or, if it's your retirement account that concerns you most, you are free to feed that now.

Assuming there was nothing criminally actionable about your departure from government, you will soon recover your old popularity. It's an odd thing the way over time the American memory makes politicians into statesmen. As a rule, the longer you are out of office, the more your community will come to regard what you did in office with reverence. You can help this process along by doing a couple of things.

Take some time off from government to put your private affairs in order. The rush of events in government and the sacrifices that must be made take their toll on our private affairs. Get a job. Become a consultant. Garden. Write a book. Travel with your family. Smell the roses.

Then re-emerge slowly. This takes political timing. But it's important. If you were for the schools when you were in office, if that's what your constituents particularly associated you with, and if that's what you want to spend some time on now, wait for a good schools issue to come up. Then get involved. If it was libraries, wait for a libraries issue.

Don't worry about your proclivity towards speaking honestly. Nurture it. Being out of office is different. It's like going back to your early days fighting highways. Now you can be an advocate again. You don't have to concern yourself with placating various constituencies. You can pick your issues again. But be careful. Everyone will want you to chair their committee. And committees take time, lots of it. Make sure you have it. Get your financial life in order first.

If you want to be a consultant and help real estate developers get their projects permitted, and there can be a lot of money in that, check the state ethics laws first. There is probably a waiting period.

There will be no waiting period if you want to go into real estate sales, although there may be some projects you should stay away from for a year or two. Again, consult the state ethics code. Your name recognition will bring you customers, especially out-of-towners.

If you have a law degree, consider becoming "of counsel" to a local law firm. The partners will trot you into various meetings to help land new clients, but besides that there's no more to it than you want there to be. You'll get an office and maybe even a secretary. And, depending upon the situation, the money can be very good.

Along the way, since by virtue of your extensive contacts with elected officials you now know them all and they know you, stay involved with their fundraising. This doesn't mean you have to give money, unless you want to. Your name will bring credibility to candidates. Helping candidates raise money will preserve your access and if you give too, may even increase your entrée to those who win. If you're good at picking winners, and by now you ought to be, a little bit of effort put forth raising money for others will further enhance your prestige within your community and help you keep getting the things done you know your community needs. If you're not sure, help both sides.

If you want a real job, associate yourself with a local insurance company. Selling insurance is a networker's dream job. And here again your name recognition will help you.

Finally, depending upon your community, there may be foundation sector work available. These jobs often leave time for other endeavors.

There are a thousand examples of former elected officials going into all these lines of work and, depending upon the sizes of their towns and how good they were as elected officials, making more money than they could have realistically dreamed of before they first ran for office.

But making lots of money probably won't be enough. It certainly will not be for those who went into government to make a difference in their communities. These will want to stay involved and, frankly, the government will in most cases want them involved. Elected officials, after they have been elected officials for a while, gain a special view of their community. They receive the benefit of innumerable staff reports. They wrestle with one another and learn from one another in the process. And since the public is empowered to communicate with them in innumerable ways, they learn a great deal from the public's comments. After a while they come to see how the whole community fits together. Next, if they're at all bright, they come to see where the community as a community is going. Few outside public life have this perspective and it is very beneficial for a community that those who do stay involved. After the passions of campaigns have died down, the sitting government may reach out to its former colleagues to chair special committees.

In my case, when the restoration of the Henry C. Chambers Waterfront Park began looming seriously on the horizon, I reached out to former councilman Jim Neighbors to chair a newly created Parks Utilization Committee. When Jim served on Council with me, he'd had a special interest in the city's parks. As chairman of the city's Parks Utilization Committee, he has put in hundreds of hours distilling the disparate views in the community into policy recommendations for the uses of the city's various parks, including the renovated Waterfront Park.

Jim's a great chairman. As a former councilman, he understands how the community fits together. He knows when to ask for a legal opinion. He knows how to run a meeting. He knows when he needs research. He knows whose ox is being gored with every recommendation his committee makes. He knows how the budget process works. He knows about the special pots of money and how they may be accessed. Moreover, he's working for free and without reelection concerns, so he can tell it like it is. And he loves doing just that.

There will be many opportunities. Choose carefully. People always ask me what Ed's doing now and I tell them that he has a TV show and a radio show, is a partner in a law firm, gives speeches, and writes movie reviews, political commentary, and books. When we talk on the phone, he is always cheerful. And there is no more prolific writer in America today. Now pushing eighty, he's as strong, forthright, and courageous as ever.

Ed has changed some pretty big political rules over the course of his estimable career. One of them was to write a tell-all political autobiography while he was still in office. That had never been done before. Most sitting mayors write about the plight of the cities, or about how the welfare system should be reformed. They never name names.

Another rule Ed changed was the one that said don't criticize your successor. Ed kept his hands off Dinkins for about six months, until the new mayor mishandled the Crown Heights racial riots. When Dinkins ran for reelection in '93, again wading in where most fear to tread, Ed supported Dinkins's challenger, Rudy Giuliani. But two years later Ed couldn't resist criticizing Giuliani when the new mayor dismantled Ed's merit selection of judges process. From there things went from bad to worse so that over the next four years Ed attacked Giuliani so regularly that Ed's publisher finally collected his anti-Giuliani columns into a book. Now, in the aftermath of the destruction of the World Trade Center and with an understanding of the wonderfully sensitive way Giuliani handled the crisis, it is hard to imagine that for the first six years of his eight years as mayor, Giuliani was a creep. Yes, he got the graffiti off the trains and the litter off Madison Avenue. But he ran his government with the sensitivity of a loan shark.

It was only after the dissolution of his marriage and his struggle with prostate cancer that, as his mayoralty was winding down, Giuliani found where his heart was. And a public official needs a heart. For government to reach down to individuals, those in charge need to be able to find their hearts. Staffers seldom will. They will advocate for policies, steamrolling the case-by-case needs of individuals time after time. Good politicians genuinely like people as individuals, not just in the abstract. No sooner had Giuliani found his heart, it seems, than fanatics brought disaster upon his city and the fates chose him for political immortality.

Now Giuliani imagines he will be president. The odds are long against him. If there is a mayor who has become president, I'm not aware of it. There's a track to the White House and mayor isn't on it. In fact being a mayor is nine times out of ten a dead end job. In his second term Robert Wagner tried to win a senate seat and lost. Lindsay wanted to be president and lost. Koch ran for governor and lost. There is a need among ambitious people to move up, although when mayors move up they move farther from the people and thus, I believe, necessarily see the results of their labors in less personal terms.

Knowing the odds, go ahead and give it a run anyway. Richard Lugar was a very good mayor of Indianapolis in the '60s and he managed to make the leap from there to the U.S. Senate where he has served admirably. Others have made similar transitions. If you lose, provided your campaign was issues-based, your legacy won't be tarnished and you can return to your well-deserved place as a senior statesman.

29. Coming Back

OCCASIONALLY

an elected official who was beaten, or who just stepped down, will come back for more. There can be no question that these campaigners have "the fire in the belly" that is so appealing to voters and that so often makes the difference between winning and losing.

One of two dynamics is usually at play in these campaigns. Both relate to the pace of change. Sometimes in his first term the official is so visionary, wants to do so many good things, that he goes too fast for his constituents and they, with the help of his next opponent, conclude he's a kook and vote him out. Then, after events have unfolded, thinking people come to conclude he wasn't kooky at all, just smart, and he is vindicated. That vindication process sets the stage for his comeback.

This was the case with former Cleveland Mayor Dennis Kucinich, who as this book was being written was running for president. In 1978 Cleveland faced bankruptcy with Kucinich, then thirty-one years old and the youngest big city mayor in the country, on the job for a year. The city's business leaders importuned Kucinich, a Democrat, to auction off the municipal electric works so that the city could make its bond payments and avert a fiscal collapse. The mayor refused and Cleveland defaulted.

The next year the voters turned Kucinich out in favor of

George Voinovich, a candidate with a more mainstream profile. Despondent, Kucinich retreated into academia and the political desert until 1993. By then Cleveland had pulled its affairs back together, in part thanks to the revenues generated by the municipal electric works, and the city's leadership had concluded that Kucinich's judgment in 1978 was the correct one. Vindicated, Kucinich returned to politics, running for the Ohio state senate in 1993. His memorable logo in that campaign was "Because he was right," with a glowing lightbulb alongside the words.

Kucinich won, and from there he jumped in 1997 to the U.S. Congress.

Beaufort County Council Vice Chairman W. R. "Skeet" Von Harten's story is a similar one, except instead of moving up Skeet sought only to be returned to an office he'd left a decade before. Von Harten was vice chairman and then chairman of the county council back in the early '90s, just after the county had completed construction of its big new government headquarters complex, widely derided as "the Taj Mahal." The local economy sagged (as a result of the national recession and the deployment at the same time of troops from this military town to the Persian Gulf to fight Saddam Hussein the first time) and county revenues faltered just when the demand for public services increased and the government was hocked up to its gills paying for the Taj. The county's response was to raise property taxes substantially several years in a row. The tax increases spawned a taxpayers group full of libertarian venom called Focus on Beaufort County.

Focus on Beaufort County's members meticulously assembled data from around the state, data that purportedly showed that Beaufort County was the most expensive and inefficiently run county government in South Carolina. They attended virtually every council meeting and bedeviled the county council, including Skeet, its chairman.

After a while, Skeet started to take their attacks personally. And he took to lecturing them, telling them that if they wanted to run the government, they should stand for election, and so on. Soon it was one man against a committee of numbers-crunching zealots. They tag-teamed him in the meetings and in the papers. Finally, still popular but weary from the fight, Skeet chose not to seek reelection.

So he returned to his full-time job and virtually disappeared off the political radar screen in Beaufort County for nearly a decade. During that time the local economy boomed, and the county recovered its financial footing. Moreover, tens of thousands of new residents flooded in, many to Sun City–Hilton Head, which Skeet had helped bring to Beaufort County in 1992, and the county's payroll had swelled to keep up with the growth. By 2001 the Taj was so full up with county employees that the county's managers were throwing out all the tenants they could, and looking for overflow quarters besides.

In those years also, a couple of heart attacks caused Skeet to spend some time in the hospital up in Charleston, long enough apparently to search his soul and determine he missed public life. The death of Councilman Pete Covington in 2002 produced a vacancy and Skeet decided to come back, winning easily. Upon his return, Council chose their former chairman, now again a freshman, to be their vice chairman. Besides Ed Koch in his prime as mayor, I don't think I have known a public official who was so contented in his job as Skeet was in his first couple of months back on the job.

The other political dynamic that is often at work when successful comebacks occur is that the voters buy into the promise of change, but then when the new ways grate, the voters buy out just as quickly as they bought in.

This was the case in the 1980s with Mayor Jimmy Anderson in Camden, South Carolina. Camden, situated in the arid Carolina midlands and featuring more than its share of antebellum mansions, became in the twentieth century a capitol of racehorse training. Thoroughbreds were sent to Camden as to a wintertime spa. At midcentury DuPont built a large chemical plant outside of town, and a bunch of Yankees moved in, joining the downtown retailers, the African-American community, and the swells from the track as Camden's significant constituencies.

In 1960 Camden elected James Anderson to be its mayor. Anderson was a big, gruff, and explosive man. The owner and operator of a local iron works, he was known locally as "The Bear." Throughout the '60s and '70s The Bear ran Camden down to the last detail. And he was good at it. It was the old style and the old style worked . . . in the old days. In theory the city was run under the council-manager form of government, which gives to councils the right to hire and fire the manager but leaves to the managers the day-to-day responsibilities for implementing the affairs of the government. In practice, in Mayor Anderson's Camden as often as not the city's agency heads took their orders directly from Anderson. Thus it was not uncommon for city workers to find themselves working on side projects in the backyards of The Bear's supporters, who for many years were most everyone in Camden. On family funeral days, Heaven forbid, they'd get the lawn mowed, courtesy of Jimmy and the parks department. If there was a tree in their yard that needed to come down, the city's workers could be counted upon to remove it, when Jimmy gave the word. The cemeteries were subsidized and maintained by the city. In those days Camden was like a family, and The Bear was its patriarch.

The old ways lasted until 1984, when local insurance agent H. Benthal Marshall, Jr., got together with some of the guys at the Rotary Club and decided it was time to bring Camden into the twentieth century. "Why can't the city government run like a business?" he asked.

Bennie, as he was known around town, was a gentle giant of a man. He was comfortable among the horseracing set. Soft-spoken but resolute, he knew most everyone and most everyone liked him. The challenge came as a surprise to the incumbent. It was over almost before it began, and The Bear was suddenly out.

After he was sworn in, Mayor Bennie started doing the things he had said he would. With school principal Mary Clark now with him on the council, Bennie and the progressives had solid control. In the face of the change, Anderson's longtime city manager left, and Bennie and his council reached out for a smart young professional who could oversee the changes Camden so badly needed. Before long they had hired Gary Cannon. With a master's in public administration from Chapel Hill, and (despite his youthful appearance) with considerable experience as a manager, Cannon was a controversial figure in Camden before he had unpacked his bags. Always dapper in his bow ties, a scratch golfer with an easy manner, Gary Cannon is a very likable man. But he is also a man in a hurry.

Together the new team set about bringing Camden into the modern age. The funeral day lawn mows were out, and computers were in. The municipal tree removal service was out, and meetings were in. Deemed too expensive and not a city problem, the cemetery maintenance program was jettisoned. Cannon hired a professional personnel director and together they authored a personnel manual for the city. That meant personnel matters would be subject to personnel policies. Camden is an electric city and the new administration also reorganized the electric utility. The city was lurching toward being run like a modern business, and the creaking and groaning and straining could be heard for miles.

By 1988 Marshall felt the city had been put on the right track. The work had been exhausting, the responsibilities had taken their toll on Bennie's family, and he declined to seek re-election. Likable or not, Bennie was more businessman than politician. And for all the rhetoric to the contrary, businessmen generally don't make very good politicians. The good ones are too despotic by nature, and the rest often irritate their constituents with their self-indulgent ways. Well-run businesses are necessarily lean, flexible, and dynamic. Decision-making in an American-style democracy with all its requisite checks and balances is as lean, flexible, and dynamic as a Rube Goldberg contraption. Businessmen often find the details of government Byzantine, and it makes them long for the private sector. Bennie was one of these.

The new ways had affected most everyone in town. Some liked them, others didn't. One group that was sure they didn't like the new ways was the city's workforce, most of whom had been hired by Anderson and had learned their jobs doing them Anderson's way. Among other things, they wanted to be treated personally, or on a case-by-case basis, and decidedly not by a personnel director with a bunch of policies and procedures. The city workforce wanted The Bear back, and quietly but with resolve they went about getting their way.

As election day approached, two sought to fill the vacancy: Anderson announced his intention to return, and the school principal, Mary Clark, announced her intention to move up. Council-man Clark said she'd continue Camden's march into the future. The Bear, for his part, didn't say much at all. He ran an old-style campaign, the kind where people talk to each other at church and in the coffee shops, the kind where men talk to men about how government's no place for a woman. In the last week no one knew anything. But when it was over The Bear was back . . . by twenty-five votes.

Gary Cannon lasted two years under The Bear, and it is a tribute to his professionalism as a manager that he did. But that was it. By 1989 he was a management consultant in Charlotte. Back in Camden, the lawn and tree services were back, and the utilities and personnel manuals were history.

Changing the ways things have been done means taking on the establishment. And the establishment has inertia for its natural ally. Changes can be made, but they must be made at a deliberate pace.

Change is organic. It must grow. It can under special circum-stances be imposed abruptly, but it must then be protected so that it may take root. For changes in the ways of governments to take root, time must be allowed so that the voters may be shown that the changes were in their interests after all.

The nutrient of change is dialogue. As in all dialogues, timing is a very important element. The public official must speak, but he must listen too. Change can be promoted by effective commu-nication and change can be halted by effective communication. Those who only speak but don't listen don't last, and the changes they have brought perish with them, though perhaps not forever.

Mary Clark is the very good mayor of Camden today. Jimmy Anderson and Bennie Marshall have each gone to their respec-tive just rewards. At city hall there are meetings and computers.

The council-manager form of government survives and thrives. And the lawn and tree services are reportedly out for good.

Out on St. Helena Island, U.S. 21 is still two lanes. There are a few more buildings there than there were a decade ago, and the schools are better. But life is much the same. And the road from Beaufort to the beach is still one of the most beautiful rides through history there is anywhere in the world.